Machine Learning wit[h] Spark Quick Start Gui[de]

Uncover patterns, derive actionable insights, and learn from big data using MLlib

Jillur Quddus

BIRMINGHAM - MUMBAI

Machine Learning with Apache Spark Quick Start Guide

Commissioning Editor: Amey Varangaonkar
Acquisition Editor: Siddharth Mandal
Content Development Editor: Mohammed Yusuf Imaratwale
Technical Editor: Diksha Wakode
Copy Editor: Safis Editing
Project Coordinator: Kinjal Bari
Proofreader: Safis Editing
Indexer: Rekha Nair
Graphics: Alishon Mendonsa
Production Coordinator: Aparna Bhagat

First published: December 2018

Production reference: 1211218

Published by Packt Publishing Ltd.
Livery Place
35 Livery Street
Birmingham
B3 2PB, UK.

ISBN 978-1-78934-656-5

www.packtpub.com

To my wife and best friend, Jane, for making life worth living. And to the memory of my parents, for their sacrifices and giving me the freedom to explore my imagination.

– Jillur Quddus

mapt.io

Mapt is an online digital library that gives you full access to over 5,000 books and videos, as well as industry leading tools to help you plan your personal development and advance your career. For more information, please visit our website.

Why subscribe?

- Spend less time learning and more time coding with practical ebooks and videos from over 4,000 industry professionals

- Improve your learning with Skill Plans built especially for you

- Get a free ebook or video every month

- Mapt is fully searchable

- Copy and paste, print, and bookmark content

Packt.com

Did you know that Packt offers ebook versions of every book published, with PDF and ePub files available? You can upgrade to the ebook version at www.packt.com and as a print book customer, you are entitled to a discount on the ebook copy. Get in touch with us at customercare@packtpub.com for more details.

At www.packt.com, you can also read a collection of free technical articles, sign up for a range of free newsletters, and receive exclusive discounts and offers on Packt books and ebooks.

Contributors

About the author

Jillur Quddus is a lead technical architect, polyglot software engineer and data scientist with over 10 years of hands-on experience in architecting and engineering distributed, scalable, high-performance, and secure solutions used to combat serious organized crime, cybercrime, and fraud. Jillur has extensive experience of working within central government, intelligence, law enforcement, and banking, and has worked across the world including in Japan, Singapore, Malaysia, Hong Kong, and New Zealand. Jillur is both the founder of Keisan, a UK-based company specializing in open source distributed technologies and machine learning, and the lead technical architect at Methods, the leading digital transformation partner for the UK public sector.

First and foremost, I would like to thank my wonderful and gorgeous wife, Jane, for all her love, support, and general awesomeness. This book, and indeed all the moments of happiness in my life, would not have been possible without her. Thank you also to my amazing brother, Gipil Quddus, and life-long friends Rie Tokuoka, Tatsuya Mukai, Nori Tokuoka and (the incredibly lovely) Shan Gao for fuelling my imagination with weird and wonderful ideas.

About the reviewer

Emmanuel Asimadi is a data scientist currently focusing on natural language processing as applied to the domain of customer experience. He has an MSc in cloud computing from the University of Leicester, UK, with over a decade experience in a variety of analytic roles both in academic research and industry. His varied portfolio includes projects in Apache Spark, natural language processing, semantic web, and telecommunications operations management involving the creation and maintenance of ETL services that support telecom infrastructure operations and maintenance using data from thousands of nodes in the field.

Emmanuel also co-authored a video called *Advanced Machine Learning with Spark* and has made a significant contribution to the development of the video *Big Data Analytics Projects with Apache Spark*, which was published recently by Packt Publishing.

> *I love everything to do with data and the value it delivers, and I feel very fortunate to be part of its creation and the first-hand experience thereof. I am a big fan of Apache Spark because of its unified approach and simple APIs, which align very well with my general philosophy of teaching – that even the most complex concepts can be explained simply – and it is great to see this applied in this book.*

Packt is searching for authors like you

If you're interested in becoming an author for Packt, please visit `authors.packtpub.com` and apply today. We have worked with thousands of developers and tech professionals, just like you, to help them share their insight with the global tech community. You can make a general application, apply for a specific hot topic that we are recruiting an author for, or submit your own idea.

Table of Contents

Preface

Every person and every organization in the world manages data, whether they realize it or not. Data is used to describe the world around us and can be used for almost any purpose, from analyzing consumer habits in order to recommend the latest products and services to fighting disease, climate change, and serious organized crime. Ultimately, we manage data in order to derive value from it, whether personal or business value, and many organizations around the world have traditionally invested in tools and technologies to help them process their data faster and more efficiently in order to deliver actionable insights.

But we now live in a highly interconnected world driven by mass data creation and consumption, where data is no longer rows and columns restricted to a spreadsheet but an organic and evolving asset in its own right. With this realization comes major challenges for organizations as we enter the intelligence-driven fourth industrial revolution—how do we manage the sheer amount of data being created every second in all of its various formats (think not only spreadsheets and databases, but also social media posts, images, videos, music, online forums and articles, computer log files, and more)? And once we know how to manage all of this data, how do we know what questions to ask of it in order to derive real personal or business value?

The focus of this book is to help us answer those questions in a hands-on manner starting from first principles. We introduce the latest cutting-edge technologies (the big data ecosystem, including Apache Spark) that can be used to manage and process big data. We then explore advanced classes of algorithms (machine learning, deep learning, natural language processing, and cognitive computing) that can be applied to the big data ecosystem to help us uncover previously hidden relationships in order to understand what the data is telling us so that we may ultimately solve real-world challenges.

Who this book is for

This book is aimed at business analysts, data analysts, data scientists, data engineers, and software engineers for whom a typical day may currently involve analyzing data using spreadsheets or relational databases, perhaps using VBA, **Structured Query Language (SQL)**, or even Python to compute statistical aggregations (such as averages) and to generate graphs, charts, pivot tables and other reporting mediums.

With the explosion of data in all of its various formats and frequencies, perhaps you are now challenged with not only managing all of that data, but understanding what it is telling you. You have most likely heard the terms **big data**, **artificial intelligence**, and **machine learning**, but now wish to understand where to start in order to take advantage of these new technologies and frameworks, not just in theory but in practice as well, to solve your business challenges. If this sounds familiar, then this book is for you!

What this book covers

Chapter 1, *The Big Data Ecosystem*, provides an introduction to the current big data ecosystem. With the multitude of on-premises and cloud-based technologies, tools, services, libraries, and frameworks available in the big data, artificial intelligence, and machine learning space (and growing every day!), it is vitally important to understand the logical function of each layer within the big data ecosystem so that we may understand how they integrate with each other in order to ultimately architect and engineer end-to-end data intelligence and machine learning pipelines. This chapter also provides a logical introduction to Apache Spark within the context of the wider big data ecosystem.

Chapter 2, *Setting Up a Local Development Environment*, provides a detailed and hands-on guide to installing, configuring, and deploying a local Linux-based development environment on your personal desktop, laptop, or cloud-based infrastructure. You will learn how to install and configure all the software services required for this book in one self-contained location, including installing and configuring prerequisite programming languages (Java JDK 8 and Python 3), a distributed data processing and analytics engine (Apache Spark 2.3), a distributed real-time streaming platform (Apache Kafka 2.0), and a web-based notebook for interactive data insights and analytics (Jupyter Notebook).

Chapter 3, *Artificial Intelligence and Machine Learning*, provides a concise theoretical summary of the various applied subjects that fall under the artificial intelligence field of study, including machine learning, deep learning, and cognitive computing. This chapter also provides a logical introduction into how end-to-end data intelligence and machine learning pipelines may be architected and engineered using Apache Spark and its machine learning library, `MLlib`.

Chapter 4, *Supervised Learning Using Apache Spark,* provides a hands-on guide to engineering, training, validating, and interpreting the results of supervised machine learning algorithms using Apache Spark through real-world use-cases. The chapter describes and implements commonly used classification and regression techniques including linear regression, logistic regression, classification and regression trees (CART), and random forests.

Chapter 5, *Unsupervised Learning Using Apache Spark,* provides a hands-on guide to engineering, training, validating, and interpreting the results of unsupervised machine learning algorithms using Apache Spark through real-world use-cases. The chapter describes and implements commonly-used unsupervised techniques including hierarchical clustering, K-means clustering, and dimensionality reduction via **Principal Component Analysis (PCA)**.

Chapter 6, *Natural Language Processing Using Apache Spark,* provides a hands-on guide to engineering **natural language processing (NLP)** pipelines using Apache Spark through real-world use-cases. The chapter describes and implements commonly used NLP techniques including tokenisation, stemming, lemmatization, normalization, and other feature transformers, and feature extractors such as the bag of words and **Term Frequency-Inverse Document Frequency (TF-IDF)** algorithms.

Chapter 7, *Deep Learning Using Apache Spark,* provides a hands-on exploration of the exciting and cutting-edge world of deep learning! The chapter uses third-party deep learning libraries in conjunction with Apache Spark to train and interpret the results of **Artificial Neural Networks (ANNs)** including **Multi-Layer Perceptrons (MLPs)** and **Convolutional Neural Networks (CNNs)** applied to real-world use-cases.

Chapter 8, *Real-Time Machine Learning Using Apache Spark,* extends the deployment of machine learning models beyond batch processing in order to learn from data, make predictions, and identify trends in real-time! The chapter provides a hands-on guide to engineering and deploying real-time stream processing and machine learning pipelines using Apache Spark and Apache Kafka to transport, transform, and analyze data streams as they are being created around the world.

To get the most out of this book

Though this book aims to explain everything from first principles, it would be advantageous (though not strictly required) to have a basic knowledge of mathematical notation and basic programming skills in a language that can be used for data transformation, such as SQL, Base SAS, R, or Python. A good website for beginners to learn about SQL and Python is https://www.w3schools.com.

It is assumed that you have access to a physical or virtual machine provisioned with the CentOS Linux 7 (or Red Hat Linux) operating system. If you do not, Chapter 2, *Setting Up a Local Development Environment*, describes the various options available to provision a CentOS 7 **virtual machine** (**VM**), including via cloud-computing platforms such as **Amazon Web Services** (**AWS**), Microsoft Azure, and **Google Cloud Platform** (**GCP**), virtual private server hosting companies or free virtualization software such as Oracle VirtualBox and VMWare Workstation Player that can be installed on your local physical device, such as a desktop or laptop.

A basic knowledge of Linux shell commands is required in order to install, configure, and provision a self-contained local development environment hosting the prerequisite software services detailed in Chapter 2, *Setting Up a Local Development Environment*. A good website for beginners to learn about the Linux command line is http://linuxcommand.org.

Download the example code files

You can download the example code files for this book from your account at www.packt.com. If you purchased this book elsewhere, you can visit www.packt.com/support and register to have the files emailed directly to you.

You can download the code files by following these steps:

1. Log in or register at www.packt.com.
2. Select the **SUPPORT** tab.
3. Click on **Code Downloads & Errata**.
4. Enter the name of the book in the **Search** box and follow the onscreen instructions.

Once the file is downloaded, please make sure that you unzip or extract the folder using the latest version of:

- WinRAR/7-Zip for Windows
- Zipeg/iZip/UnRarX for Mac
- 7-Zip/PeaZip for Linux

The code bundle for the book is also hosted on GitHub at `https://github.com/PacktPublishing/Machine-Learning-with-Apache-Spark-Quick-Start-Guide`. In case there's an update to the code, it will be updated on the existing GitHub repository.

We also have other code bundles from our rich catalog of books and videos available at `https://github.com/PacktPublishing/`. Check them out!

Conventions used

There are a number of text conventions used throughout this book.

`CodeInText`: Indicates code words in text, database table names, folder names, filenames, file extensions, pathnames, dummy URLs, user input, and Twitter handles. Here is an example: "Mount the downloaded `WebStorm-10*.dmg` disk image file as another disk in your system."

A block of code is set as follows:

```
import findspark
findspark.init()
from pyspark import SparkContext, SparkConf
import random
```

Any command-line input or output is written as follows:

```
> source /etc/profile.d/java.sh
> echo $PATH
> echo $JAVA_HOME
```

Bold: Indicates a new term, an important word, or words that you see onscreen. For example, words in menus or dialog boxes appear in the text like this. Here is an example: "Select **System info** from the **Administration** panel."

Warnings or important notes appear like this.

Tips and tricks appear like this.

Get in touch

Feedback from our readers is always welcome.

General feedback: If you have questions about any aspect of this book, mention the book title in the subject of your message and email us at customercare@packtpub.com.

Errata: Although we have taken every care to ensure the accuracy of our content, mistakes do happen. If you have found a mistake in this book, we would be grateful if you would report this to us. Please visit www.packt.com/submit-errata, selecting your book, clicking on the Errata Submission Form link, and entering the details.

Piracy: If you come across any illegal copies of our works in any form on the Internet, we would be grateful if you would provide us with the location address or website name. Please contact us at copyright@packt.com with a link to the material.

If you are interested in becoming an author: If there is a topic that you have expertise in and you are interested in either writing or contributing to a book, please visit authors.packtpub.com.

Reviews

Please leave a review. Once you have read and used this book, why not leave a review on the site that you purchased it from? Potential readers can then see and use your unbiased opinion to make purchase decisions, we at Packt can understand what you think about our products, and our authors can see your feedback on their book. Thank you!

For more information about Packt, please visit packt.com.

1
The Big Data Ecosystem

Modern technology has transformed the very essence of what we mean by data. Whereas previously, data was traditionally thought of as text and numbers confined to spreadsheets or relational databases, today, it is an organic and evolving asset in its own right, being created and consumed on a mass scale by anyone that owns a smartphone, TV, or bank account. In this chapter, we will explore the new ecosystem of cutting-edge tools, technologies, and frameworks that allow us to store, process, and analyze massive volumes of data in order to deliver actionable insights and solve real-world problems. By the end of this chapter, you will have gained a high-level understanding of the following cutting-edge technology classes:

- Distributed systems
- NoSQL databases
- Artificial intelligence and machine learning frameworks
- Cloud computing platforms
- Big data platforms and reference architecture

A brief history of data

If you worked in the mainstream IT industry between the 1970s and early 2000s, it is likely that your organization's data was held either in text-based delimited files, spreadsheets, or nicely structured relational databases. In the case of the latter, data is modeled and persisted in pre-defined, and possibly related, tables representing the various entities found within your organization's data model, for example, according to employee or department. These tables contain rows of data across multiple columns representing the various attributes making up that entity; for example, in the case of employee, typical attributes include first name, last name, and date of birth.

Vertical scaling

As both your organization's data estate and the number of users requiring access to that data grew, high-performance remote servers would have been utilized, with access provisioned over the corporate network. These remote servers would typically either act as remote filesystems for file sharing or host **relational database management systems** (**RDBMSes**) in order to store and manage relational databases. As data requirements grew, these remote servers would have needed to scale vertically, meaning that additional CPU, memory, and/or hard disk space would have been installed. Typically, these relational databases would have stored anything between hundreds and potentially tens of millions of records.

Master/slave architecture

As a means of providing resilience and load balancing read requests, potentially, a master/slave architecture would have been employed whereby data is automatically copied from the master database server to physically distinct slave database server(s) utilizing near real-time replication. This technique requires that the master server be responsible for all write requests, while read requests could be offloaded and load balanced across the slaves, where each slave would hold a full copy of the master data. That way, if the master server ever failed for some reason, business-critical read requests could still be processed by the slaves while the master was being brought back online. This technique does have a couple of major disadvantages, however:

- **Scalability**: The master server, by being solely responsible for processing write requests, limits the ability for the system to be scalable as it could quickly become a bottleneck.
- **Consistency and data loss**: Since replication is near real-time, it is not guaranteed that the slaves would have the latest data at the point in time that the master server goes offline and transactions may be lost. Depending on the business application, either not having the latest data or losing data may be unacceptable.

Sharding

To increase throughput and overall performance, and as single machines reached their capacity to scale vertically in a cost-effective manner, it is possible that sharding would have been employed. This is one method of horizontal scaling whereby additional servers are provisioned and data is physically split over separate database instances residing on each of the machines in the cluster, as illustrated in *Figure 1.1*.

This approach would have allowed organizations to scale linearly to cater for increased data sizes while reusing existing database technologies and commodity hardware, thereby optimizing costs and performance for small- to medium-sized databases.

Crucially, however, these separate databases are standalone instances and have no knowledge of one another. Therefore, some sort of broker would be required that, based on a partitioning strategy, would keep track of where data was being written to for each write request and, thereafter, retrieve data from that same location for read requests. Sharding subsequently introduced further challenges, such as processing data queries, transformations, and joins that spanned multiple standalone database instances across multiple servers (without denormalizing data), thereby maintaining referential integrity and the repartitioning of data:

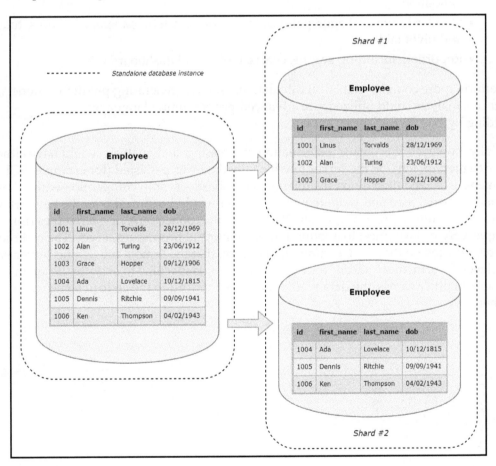

Figure 1.1: A simple sharding partitioning strategy

Data processing and analysis

Finally, in order to transform, process, and analyze the data sitting in these delimited text-based files, spreadsheets or relational databases, typically an analyst, data engineer or software engineer would have written some code.

This code, for example, could take the form of formulas or **Visual Basic for Applications** (**VBA**) for spreadsheets, or **Structured Query Language** (**SQL**) for relational databases, and would be used for the following purposes:

- Loading data, including batch loading and data migration
- Transforming data, including data cleansing, joins, merges, enrichment, and validation
- Standard statistical aggregations, including computing averages, counts, totals, and pivot tables
- Reporting, including graphs, charts, tables, and dashboards

To perform more complex statistical calculations, such as generating predictive models, advanced analysts could utilize more advanced programming languages, including Python, R, SAS, or even Java.

Crucially, however, this data transformation, processing, and analysis would have either been executed directly on the server in which the data was persisted (for example, SQL statements executed directly on the relational database server in competition with other business-as-usual read and write requests), or data would be moved over the network via a programmatic query (for example, an ODBC or JDBC connection), or via flat files (for example, CSV or XML files) to another remote analytical processing server. The code could then be executed on that data, assuming, of course, that the remote processing server had sufficient CPUs, memory and/or disk space in its single machine to execute the job in question. In other words, the data would have been moved to the code in some way or another.

Data becomes big

Fast forward to today—spreadsheets are still commonplace, and relational databases containing nicely structured data, whether partitioned across shards or not, are still very much relevant and extremely useful. In fact, depending on the use case, the data volumes, structure, and the computational complexity of the required processing, it could still be faster and more efficient to store and manage data via an RDBMS and process that data directly on the remote database server using SQL. And, of course, spreadsheets are still great for very small datasets and for simple statistical aggregations. What has changed, however, since the 1970s is the availability of more powerful and more cost-effective technology coupled with the introduction of the internet!

The internet has transformed the very essence of what we mean by data. Whereas before, data was thought of as text and numbers confined to spreadsheets or relational databases, it is now an organic and evolving asset in its own right being created and consumed on a mass scale by anyone that owns a smartphone, TV, or bank account. Data is being created every second around the world in virtually any format you can think of, from social media posts, images, videos, audio, and music to blog posts, online forums, articles, computer log files, and financial transactions. All of this structured, semi-structured, and unstructured data being created in both batch and real time can no longer be stored and managed by nicely organized, text-based delimited files, spreadsheets, or relational databases, nor can it *all* be physically moved to a remote processing server every time some analytical code is to be executed—a new breed of technology is required.

Big data ecosystem

If you work in almost any mainstream industry today, chances are that you may have heard of some of the following terms and phrases:

- Big data
- Distributed, scalable, and elastic
- On-premise versus the cloud
- SQL versus NoSQL
- Artificial intelligence, machine learning, and deep learning

But what do all these terms and phrases actually mean, how do they all fit together, and where do you start? The aim of this section is to answer all of those questions in a clear and concise manner.

Horizontal scaling

First of all, let's return to some of the data-centric problems that we described earlier. Given the huge explosion in the mass creation and consumption of data today, clearly we cannot continue to keep adding CPUs, memory, and/or hard drives to a single machine (in other words, vertical scaling). If we did, there would very quickly come a point where migrating to more powerful hardware would lead to diminishing returns while incurring significant costs. Furthermore, the ability to scale would be physically bounded by the biggest machine available to us, thereby limiting the growth potential of an organization.

Horizontal scaling, of which sharding is an example, is the process by which we can increase or decrease the amount of computational resources available to us via the addition or removal of hardware and/or software. Typically, this would involve the addition (or removal) of servers or nodes to a cluster of nodes. Crucially, however, the cluster acts as a single logical unit at all times, meaning that it will still continue to function and process requests regardless of whether resources were being added to it or taken away. The difference between horizontal and vertical scaling is illustrated in *Figure 1.2*:

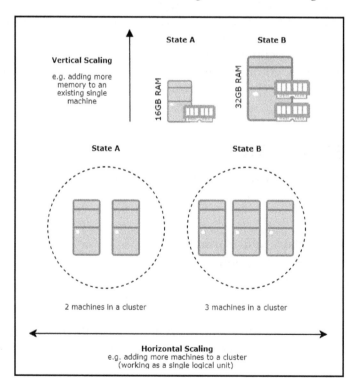

Figure 1.2: Vertical scaling versus horizontal scaling

Distributed systems

Horizontal scaling allows organizations to become much more cost efficient when data and processing requirements grow beyond a certain point. But simply adding more machines to a cluster would not be of much value by itself. What we now need are systems that are capable of taking advantage of horizontal scalability and that work across multiple machines seamlessly, irrespective of whether the cluster contains one machine or 10,000 machines.

Distributed systems do precisely that—they work seamlessly across a cluster of machines and automatically deal with the addition (or removal) of resources from that cluster. Distributed systems can be broken down into the following types:

- Distributed filesystems
- Distributed databases
- Distributed processing
- Distributed messaging
- Distributed streaming
- Distributed ledgers

Distributed data stores

Let's return to the problems faced by a single-machine RDBMS. We have seen how sharding can be employed as one method to scale relational databases horizontally in order to optimize costs as data grows for small- to medium-sized databases. However, the issue with sharding is that each node acts in a standalone manner with no knowledge of the other nodes in the cluster, meaning that a custom broker is required to both partition the data across the shards and to process read and write requests.

Distributed data stores, on the other hand, work out of the box as a single logical unit spanning a cluster of nodes.

 Note that a data store is just a general term used to describe any type of repository used to persist data. Distributed data stores extend this by storing data on more than one node, and often employ replication.

Client applications view the distributed data store as a single entity, meaning that no matter which node in the cluster physically handles the client request, the same results will be returned. Distributed filesystems, such as the **Apache Hadoop Distributed File System** (**HDFS**) discussed in the next section, belong to the class of distributed data stores and are used to store files in their raw format. When data needs to be modeled in some manner, then distributed databases can be used. Depending on the type of distributed database, it can either be deployed on top of a distributed filesystem or not.

Distributed filesystems

Think of the hard drive inside your desktop, laptop, smartphone, or other personal device you own. Files are written to and stored on local hard drives and retrieved as and when you need them. Your local operating system manages read and write requests to your local hard drive by maintaining a local filesystem—a means by which the operating system keeps track of how the disk is organized and where files are located.

As your personal data footprint grows, you take up more and more space on your local hard drive until it reaches its capacity. At this time, you may seek to purchase a larger capacity hard drive to replace the one inside your device, or you may seek to purchase an extra hard drive to complement your existing one. In the case of the latter, you personally manage which of your personal files reside on which hard drive, or perhaps use one of them to archive files you rarely use to free up space on your primary drive. Hopefully, you also maintain backups of your personal files should the worse happen and your device or primary hard drive malfunctions!

A **distributed filesystem** (**DFS**) extends the notion of local filesystems, while offering a number of useful benefits. In a distributed filesystem within the context of our big data ecosystem, data is physically split across the nodes and disks in a cluster. Like distributed data stores in general, a distributed filesystem provides a layer of abstraction and manages read and write requests across the cluster itself, meaning that the physical split is invisible to requesting client applications which view the distributed filesystem as one logical entity just like a conventional local filesystem.

Furthermore, distributed filesystems provide useful benefits out of the box, including the following:

- Data replication, where data can be configured to be automatically replicated across the cluster for fault tolerance in the event one or more of the nodes or disks should fail
- Data integrity checking
- The ability to persist huge files, typically **gigabytes (GB)** to **terabytes (TB)** in size, which would not normally be possible on conventional local filesystems

The HDFS is a well-known example of a distributed filesystem within the context of our big data ecosystem. In the HDFS, a master/slave architecture is employed, consisting of a single NameNode that manages the distributed filesystem, and multiple DataNodes, which typically reside on each node in the cluster and manage the physical disks attached to that node as well as where the data is physically persisted to. Just as with traditional filesystems, HDFS supports standard filesystem operations, such as opening and closing files and directories. When a client application requests a file to be written to the HDFS, it is split into one or more blocks that are then mapped by the NameNode to the DataNodes, where they are physically persisted. When a client application requests a file to be read from the HDFS, the DataNodes fulfill this request.

One of the core benefits of HDFS is that it provides fault tolerance inherently through its distributed architecture, as well as through data replication. Since typically there will be multiple nodes (potentially thousands) in an HDFS cluster, it is resilient to hardware failure as operations can be automatically offloaded to the healthy parts of the cluster while the non-functional hardware is being recovered or replaced. Furthermore, when a file is split into blocks and mapped by the NameNode to the DataNodes, these blocks can be configured to automatically replicate across the DataNodes, taking into account the topology of the HDFS cluster.

Therefore, if a failure did occur, for example, a disk failure on one of the DataNodes, data would still be available to client applications. The high-level architecture of an HDFS cluster is illustrated in *Figure 1.3*:

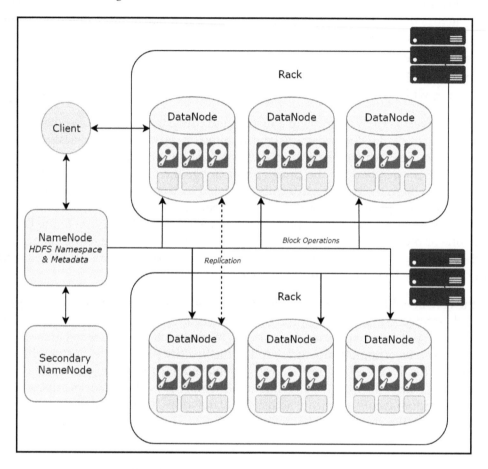

Figure 1.3: Apache Hadoop distributed filesystem high-level architecture

To learn more about the Apache Hadoop framework, please visit `http://hadoop.apache.org/`.

Distributed databases

Distributed filesystems, like conventional filesystems, are used to store files. In the case of distributed filesystems such as the HDFS, these files can be very large. Ultimately, however, they are used to store files. When data requires modeling, we need something more than just a filesystem; we need a database.

Distributed databases, just like single-machine databases, allow us to model our data. Unlike single-machine databases, however, the data, and the data model itself, spans, and is preserved across, all the nodes in a cluster acting as a single logical database. This means that not only can we take advantage of the increased performance, throughput, fault tolerance, resilience, and cost-effectiveness offered by distributed systems, but we can also model our data and thereafter query that data efficiently, no matter how large it is or how complex the processing requirements are. Depending on the type of distributed database, it can either be deployed on top of a distributed filesystem (such as Apache HBase deployed on top of the HDFS) or not.

In our big data ecosystem, it is often the case that distributed filesystems such as the HDFS are used to host **data lakes**. A data lake is a centralized data repository where data is persisted in its original raw format, such as files and object BLOBs. This allows organizations to consolidate their disparate raw data estate, including structured and unstructured data, into a central repository with no predefined schema, while offering the ability to scale over time in a cost-effective manner.

Thereafter, in order to actually deliver business value and actionable insight from this vast repository of schema-less data, data processing pipelines are engineered to transform this raw data into meaningful data conforming to some sort of data model that is then persisted into serving or analytical data stores typically hosted by distributed databases. These distributed databases are optimized, depending on the data model and type of business application, to efficiently query the large volumes of data held within them in order to serve user-facing **business intelligence** (**BI**), data discovery, advanced analytics, and insights-driven applications and APIs.

Examples of distributed databases include the following:

- Apache HBase: https://hbase.apache.org/
- Apache Cassandra: http://cassandra.apache.org/
- Apache CouchDB: http://couchdb.apache.org/
- Apache Ignite: https://ignite.apache.org/
- Greenplum Database: https://greenplum.org/
- MongoDB: https://www.mongodb.com/

Apache Cassandra is an example of a distributed database that employs a masterless architecture with no single point of failure that supports high throughput in processing huge volumes of data. In Cassandra, there is no master copy of the data. Instead, data is automatically partitioned, based on partitioning keys and other features inherent to how Cassandra models and stores data, and replicated, based on a configurable replication factor, across other nodes in the cluster. Since the concept of master/slave does not exist, a gossip protocol is employed so that the nodes in the Cassandra cluster may dynamically learn about the state and health of other nodes.

In order to process read and write requests from a client application, Cassandra will automatically elect a coordinator node from the available nodes in the cluster, a process that is invisible to the client. To process write requests, the coordinator node will, based on the partitioning features of the underlying distributed data model employed by Cassandra, contact all applicable nodes where the write request and replicas should be persisted to. To process read requests, the coordinator node will contact one or more of the replica nodes where it knows the data in question has been written to, again based on the partitioning features of Cassandra. The underlying architecture employed by Cassandra can therefore be visualized as a ring, as illustrated in *Figure 1.4*. Note that although the topology of a Cassandra cluster can be visualized as a ring, that does not mean that a failure in one node results in the failure of the entire cluster. If a node becomes unavailable for whatever reason, Cassandra will simply continue to write to the other applicable nodes that should persist the requested data, while maintaining a queue of operations pertaining to the failed node. When the non-functional node is brought back online, Cassandra will automatically update it:

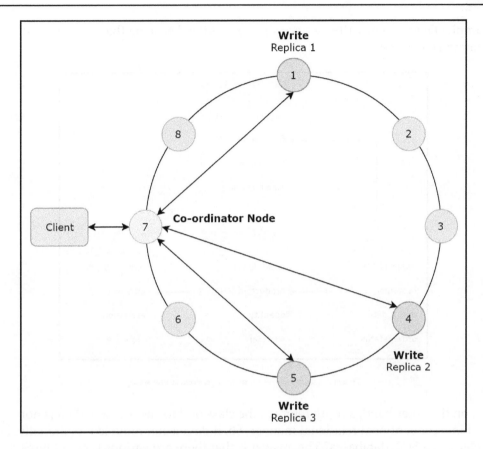

Figure 1.4: Cassandra topology illustrating a write request with a replication factor of 3

NoSQL databases

Relational Database Management Systems, such as Microsoft SQL Server, PostgreSQL, and MySQL, allow us to model our data in a structured manner across tables that represent the entities found in our data model that may be identified by primary keys and linked to other entities via foreign keys. These tables are pre-defined, with a schema consisting of columns of various data types that represent the attributes of the entity in question.

For example, *Figure 1.5* describes a very simple relational schema that could be utilized by an e-commerce website:

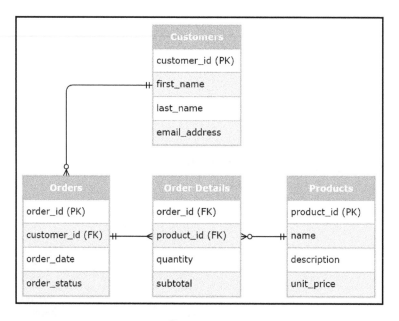

Figure 1.5: A simple relational database model for an e-commerce website

NoSQL, on the other hand, simply refers to the class of databases where data is not modeled in a conventional relational manner. So, if data is not modeled relationally, how is it modeled in NoSQL databases? The answer is that there are various types of NoSQL databases depending on the use case and business application in question. These various types are summarized in the following sub-sections.

It is a common, but mistaken, assumption that NoSQL is a synonym for distributed databases. In fact, there is an ever increasing list of RDBMS vendors whose products are designed to be scalable and distributed to accommodate huge volumes of structured data. The reason that this mistaken assumption arose is because it is often the case in real-world implementations that NoSQL databases are used to persist huge amounts of structured, semi-structured, and unstructured data in a distributed manner, hence the reason they have become synonymous with distributed databases. However, like relational databases, NoSQL databases are designed to work even on a single machine. It is the way that data is modeled that distinguishes relational, or SQL, databases from NoSQL databases.

Document databases

Document databases, such as **Apache CouchDB** and **MongoDB**, employ a document data model to store semi-structured and unstructured data. In this model, a document is used to encapsulate all the information pertaining to an object, usually in **JavaScript Object Notation (JSON)** format, meaning that a single document is self-describing. Since they are self-describing, different documents may have different schema. For example a document describing a movie item, as illustrated in the following JSON file, would have a different schema from a document describing a book item:

```
[
    {
        "title" : "The Imitation Game",
        "year": 2014
        "metadata" : {
            "directors" : [ "Morten Tyldum"],
            "release_date" : "2014-11-14T00:00:00Z",
            "rating" : 8.0,
            "genres" : ["Biography", "Drama", "Thriller"],
            "actors" : ["Benedict Cumberbatch", "Keira Knightley"]
        }
    }
]
```

Because documents are self-contained representations of objects, they are particularly useful for data models in which individual objects are updated frequently, thereby avoiding the need to update the entire database schema, as would be required with relational databases. Therefore, document databases tend to be ideal for use cases involving catalogs of items, for example e-commerce websites, and content management systems such as blogging platforms.

Columnar databases

Relational databases traditionally persist each row of data contiguously, meaning that each row will be stored in sequential blocks on disk. This type of database is referred to as *row-oriented*. For operations involving typical statistical aggregations such as calculating the average of a particular attribute, the effect of row-oriented databases is that every attribute in that row is read during processing, regardless of whether they are relevant to the query or not. In general, row-oriented databases are best suited for transactional workloads, also known as **online transaction processing (OLTP)**, where individual rows are frequently written to and where the emphasis is on processing a large number of relatively simple queries, such as short inserts and updates, quickly. Examples of use cases include retail and financial transactions where database schemas tend to be highly normalized.

On the other hand, columnar databases such as **Apache Cassandra** and **Apache HBase** are *column-oriented*, meaning that each column is persisted in sequential blocks on disk. The effect of column-oriented databases is that individual attributes can be accessed together as a group, rather than individually by row, thereby reducing disk I/O for analytical queries since the amount of data that is loaded from disk is reduced. For example, consider the following table:

Product ID	Name	Category	Unit price
1001	USB drive 64 GB	Storage	25.00
1002	SATA HDD 1 TB	Storage	50.00
1003	SSD 256 GB	Storage	60.00

In a row-oriented database, the data is persisted to disk as follows:

(1001, USB drive 64 GB, storage, 25.00), (1002, SATA HDD 1 TB, storage, 50.00), (1003, SSD 256 GB, storage, 60.00)

However, in a column-oriented database, the data is persisted to disk as follows:

(1001, 1002, 1003), (USB drive 64 GB, SATA HDD 1 TB, SSD 256 GB), (storage, storage, storage), (25.00, 50.00, 60.00)

In general, column-oriented databases are best suited for analytical workloads, also known as **online analytical processing (OLAP)**, where the emphasis is on processing a low number of complex analytical queries typically involving aggregations. Examples of use cases include data mining and statistical analysis, where database schemas tend to be either denormalized or follow a star or snowflake schema design.

Key-value databases

Key-value databases, such as **Redis**, **Oracle Berkley DB**, and **Voldemort**, employ a simple key-value data model to store data as a collection of unique keys mapped to value objects. This is illustrated in the following table that maps session IDs for web applications to session data:

Key (session ID)	Value (session data)
`ab2e66d47a04798`	`{userId: "user1", ip: "75.100.144.28", date: "2018-09-28"}`
`62f6nhd47a04dshj`	`{userId: "user2", ip: "77.189.90.26", date: "2018-09-29"}`
`83hbnndtw3e6388`	`{userId: "user3", ip: "73.43.181.201", date: "2018-09-30"}`

Key-value data structures are found in many programming languages where they are commonly referred to as *dictionaries* or *hash maps*. Key-value databases extend these data structures through their ability to partition and scale horizontally across a cluster, thereby effectively providing huge distributed dictionaries. Key-value databases are particularly useful as a means to improve the performance and throughput of systems that are required to handle potentially millions of requests per second. Examples of use cases include popular e-commerce websites, storing session data for web applications, and facilitating caching layers.

Graph databases

Graph databases, such as **Neo4j** and **OrientDB**, model data as a collection of vertices (also called nodes) linked together by one or more edges (also called relationships or links). In real-world graph implementations, vertices are often used to represent real-world entities such as individuals, organizations, vehicles, and addresses. Edges are then used to represent relationships between vertices.

Both vertices and edges can have an arbitrary number of key-value pairs, called *properties*, associated with them. For example, properties associated with an individual vertex may include a name and date of birth. Properties associated with an edge linking an individual vertex with another individual vertex may include the nature and length of the personal relationship. The collection of vertices, edges, and properties together form a data structure called a **property graph**. *Figure 1.6* illustrates a simple property graph representing a small social network:

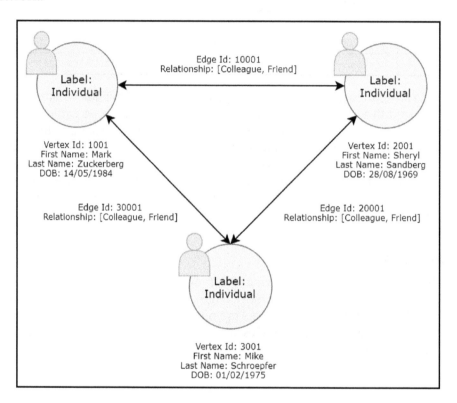

Figure 1.6: A simple property graph

Graph databases are employed in a wide variety of scenarios where the emphasis is on analyzing the relationships between objects rather than just the object's data attributes themselves. Common use cases include social network analysis, fraud detection, combating serious organized crime, customer recommendation systems, complex reasoning, pattern recognition, blockchain analysis, cyber security, and network intrusion detection.

Apache TinkerPop is an example of a graph computing framework that provides a layer of abstraction between the graph data model and the underlying mechanisms used to store and process graphs. For example, Apache TinkerPop can be used in conjunction with an underlying Apache Cassandra or Apache HBase database to store huge distributed graphs containing billions of vertices and edges partitioned across a cluster. A graph traversal language called **Gremlin**, a component of the Apache TinkerPop framework, can then be used to traverse and analyze the distributed graph using one of the Gremlin language variants including Gremlin Java, Gremlin Python, Gremlin Scala, and Gremlin JavaScript. To learn more about the Apache TinkerPop framework, please visit `http://tinkerpop.apache.org/`.

CAP theorem

As discussed previously, distributed data stores allow us to store huge volumes of data while providing the ability to horizontally scale as a single logical unit at all times. Inherent to many distributed data stores are the following features:

- **Consistency** refers to the guarantee that every client has the same view of the data. In practice, this means that a read request to any node in the cluster should return the results of the most recent successful write request. Immediate consistency refers to the guarantee that the most recent successful write request should be immediately available to any client.
- **Availability** refers to the guarantee that the system responds to every request made by a client, whether that request was successful or not. In practice, this means that every client request receives a response regardless of whether individual nodes are non-functional.
- **Partition tolerance** refers to the guarantee of resilience given a failure in inter-node network communication. In other words, in the event that there is a network failure between a particular node and another set of nodes, referred to as a network partition, the system will continue to function. In practice, this means that the system should have the ability to replicate data across the functional parts of the cluster to cater for intermittent network failures and in order to guarantee that data is not lost. Thereafter, the system should heal gracefully once the partition has been resolved.

The CAP theorem simply states that a distributed system cannot simultaneously be immediately consistent, available, and partition-tolerant. A distributed system can simultaneously only ever offer any two of the three. This is illustrated in *Figure 1.7*:

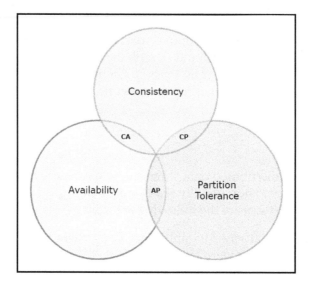

Figure 1.7: The CAP theorem

CA distributed systems offer immediate consistency and high availability, but are not tolerant to inter-node network failure, meaning that data could be lost. **CP** distributed systems offer immediate consistency and are resilient to network failure, with no data loss. However, they may not respond in the event of an inter-node network failure. **AP** distributed systems offer high availability and resilience to network failure with no data loss. However, read requests may not return the most recent data.

Distributed systems, such as Apache Cassandra, allow for the configuration of the level of consistency required. For example, let's assume we have provisioned an Apache Cassandra cluster with a replication factor of 3. In Apache Cassandra, a consistency configuration of **ONE** means that a write request is considered successful as soon as *one* copy of the data is persisted, without the need to wait for the other two replicas to be written. In this case, the system is said to be eventually consistent, as the other two replicas will eventually be persisted. A subsequent and immediate read request may either return the latest data if it is processed by the updated replica, or it may return outdated data if it is processed by one of the other two replicas that have yet to be updated (but will eventually be). In this scenario, Cassandra is an AP distributed system exhibiting eventual consistency and the tolerance of all but one of the replicas failing. It also provides the fastest performing system in this context.

A consistency configuration of **ALL** in Apache Cassandra means that a write request is considered successful only if all replicas are persisted successfully. A subsequent and immediate read request will always return the latest data. In this scenario, Cassandra is a CA distributed system exhibiting immediate consistency, but with no tolerance of failure. It also provides the slowest performing system in this context.

Finally, a consistency configuration of **QUORUM** in Apache Cassandra means that a write request is considered successful only when a strict majority of replicas are persisted successfully. A subsequent and immediate read request also using QUORUM consistency will wait until data from two replicas (in the case of a replication factor of 3) is received and, by comparing timestamps, will always return the latest data. In this scenario, Cassandra is also a CA distributed system exhibiting immediate consistency, but with the tolerance of a minority of the replicas failing. It also provides a median-performing system in this context.

Ultimately, in the real world, however, data loss is not an option for most business critical systems and a trade-off between performance, consistency and availability is required. Therefore, the choice tends to come down to either CP or AP distributed systems, with the winner driven by business requirements.

Distributed search engines

Distributed search engines, such as **Elasticsearch** based on **Apache Lucene**, transform data into highly-optimized data structures for quick and efficient searching and analysis. In Apache Lucene, data is indexed into documents containing one or more fields representing analyzed data attributes of various data types. A collection of documents forms an index, and it is this index that is searched when queries are processed, returning the relevant documents that fulfill the query. A suitable analogy would be when trying to find pages relating to a specific topic in a textbook. Instead of searching every page one by one, the reader may instead use the index at the back of the book to find relevant pages quicker. To learn more about Apache Lucene, please visit `http://lucene.apache.org/`.

Elasticsearch extends Apache Lucene by offering the ability to partition and horizontally scale search indexes and analytical queries over a distributed cluster, coupled with a RESTful search engine and HTTP web interface for high-performance searching and analysis. To learn more about Elasticsearch, please visit `https://www.elastic.co/products/elasticsearch`.

Distributed processing

We have seen how distributed data stores such as the HDFS and Apache Cassandra allow us to store and model huge volumes of structured, semi-structured, and unstructured data partitioned over horizontally scalable clusters providing fault tolerance, resilience, high availability, and consistency. But in order to provide actionable insights and to deliver meaningful business value, we now need to be able to process and analyze all that data.

Let's return to the traditional data processing scenario we described near the start of this chapter. Typically, the data transformation and analytical programming code written by an analyst, data engineer or software engineer (for example, in SQL, Python, R or SAS) would rely upon the input data to be physically moved to the remote processing server or machine where the code to be executed resided. This would often take the form of a programmatic query embedded inside the code itself, for example, a SQL statement via an ODBC or JDBC connection, or via flat files such as CSV and XML files moved to the local filesystem. Although this approach works fine for small- to medium-sized datasets, there is a physical limit bounded by the computational resources available to the single remote processing server. Furthermore, the introduction of flat files such as CSV or XML files, introduces an additional, and often unnecessary, intermediate data store that requires management and increases disk I/O.

The major problem with this approach, however, is that the data needs to be moved to the code every time a job is executed. This very quickly becomes impractical when dealing with increased data volumes and frequencies, such as the volumes and frequencies we associate with big data.

We therefore need another data processing and programming paradigm—one where code is moved to the data and that works across a distributed cluster. In other words, we require distributed processing!

The fundamental idea behind distributed processing is the concept of splitting a computational processing task into smaller tasks. These smaller tasks are then distributed across the cluster and process specific partitions of the data. Typically, the computational tasks are co-located on the same nodes as the data itself to increase performance and reduce network I/O. The results from each of the smaller tasks are then aggregated in some manner before the final result is returned.

MapReduce

MapReduce is an example of a distributed data processing paradigm capable of processing big data in parallel across a cluster of nodes. A MapReduce job splits a large dataset into independent chunks and consists of two stages—the first stage is the Map function that creates a map task for each range in the input, outputting a partitioned group of key-value pairs. The output of the map tasks then act as inputs to reduce tasks, whose job it is to combine and condense the relevant partitions in order to solve the analytical problem. Before beginning the map stage, data is often sorted or filtered based on some condition pertinent to the analysis being undertaken. Similarly, the output of the reduce function may be subject to a finalization function to further analyze the data.

Let's consider a simple example to bring this rather abstract definition to life. The example that we will consider is that of a word count. Suppose that we have a text file containing millions of lines of text, and we wish to count the number of occurrences of each unique word in this text file as a whole. *Figure 1.8* illustrates how this analysis may be undertaken using the MapReduce paradigm:

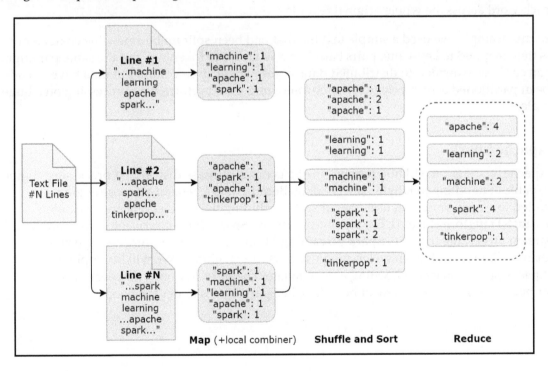

Figure 1.8: Word count MapReduce program

In this example, the original text file containing millions of lines of text is split up into its individual lines. Map tasks are applied to ranges of those individual lines, splitting them into individual word tokens, in this case, using a whitespace tokenizer, and thereafter emitting a collection of key-value pairs where the key is the word.

A *shuffling* process is undertaken that transfers the partitioned key-value pairs emitted by the map tasks to the reduce tasks. Sorting of the key-value pairs, grouped by key, is also undertaken. This helps to identify when a new reduce task should start. To reduce the amount of data transferred from the map tasks to the reduce tasks during shuffling, an optional combiner may be specified that implements a local aggregation function. In this example, a combiner is specified that sums, locally, the number of occurrences of each key or word for each map output.

The reduce tasks then take those partitioned key-value pairs and reduce those values that share the same key, outputting new (but unsorted) key-value pairs unique by key. In this example, the reduce tasks simply sum the number of occurrences of that key. The final output of the MapReduce job in this case is simply a count of the number occurrences of each word across the whole original text file.

In this example, we used a simple text file that had been split up by a newline character that is then mapped to key-value pairs based on a whitespace tokenizer. But the same paradigm can easily be extended to distributed data stores, where large volumes of data have already been partitioned across a cluster, thereby allowing us to perform data processing on a huge scale.

Apache Spark

Apache Spark is a well-known example of a general-purpose distributed processing engine capable of handling **petabytes** (**PB**) of data. Because it is a general-purpose engine, it is suited to a wide variety of use cases at scale, including the engineering and execution of **Extract-Transform-Load** (**ETL**) pipelines using its **Spark SQL** library, interactive analytics, stream processing using its **Spark Streaming** library, graph-based processing using its GraphX library, and machine learning using its MLlib library. We will be employing Apache Spark's machine learning library in later chapters. For now, however, it is important to get an overview of how Apache Spark works under the hood.

Apache Spark software services run in **Java Virtual Machines** (**JVM**), but that does not mean Spark applications must be written in Java. In fact, Spark exposes its API and programming model to a variety of language variants, including Java, Scala, Python, and R, any of which may be used to write a Spark application. In terms of its logical architecture, Spark employs a master/worker architecture as illustrated in *Figure 1.9*:

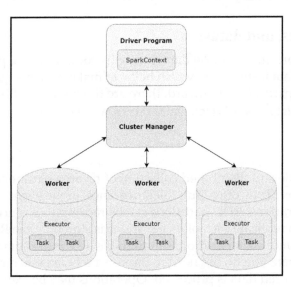

Figure 1.9: Apache Spark logical architecture

Every application written in Apache Spark consists of a **Driver Program**. The driver program is responsible for splitting a Spark application into tasks, which are then partitioned across the **Worker** nodes in the distributed cluster and scheduled to execute by the driver. The driver program also instantiates a **SparkContext**, which tells the application how to connect to the Spark cluster and its underlying services.

The worker nodes, also known as slaves, are where the computational processing physically occurs. Typically, Spark worker nodes are co-located on the same nodes as where the underlying data is also persisted to improve performance. Worker nodes spawn processes called **Executors**, and it is these executors that are responsible for executing the computational tasks and storing any locally-cached data. Executors communicate with the driver program in order to receive scheduled functions, such as map and reduce functions, which are then executed. The **Cluster Manager** is responsible for scheduling and allocating resources across the cluster and must therefore be able to communicate with every worker node, as well as the driver. The driver program requests executors from the cluster manager (since the cluster manager is aware of the resources available) so that it may schedule tasks.

Apache Spark is bundled with its own simple cluster manager which, when used, is referred to as Spark Standalone mode. Spark applications deployed to a standalone cluster will, by default, utilize all nodes in the cluster and are scheduled in a **First-In-First-Out** (**FIFO**) manner. Apache Spark also supports other cluster managers, including **Apache Mesos** and **Apache Hadoop YARN**, both of which are beyond the scope of this book.

RDDs, DataFrames, and datasets

So how does Spark store and partition data during its computational processing? Well, by default, Spark holds data in-memory, which helps to make it such a quick processing engine. In fact, as of Spark 2.0 and onward, there are three sets of APIs used to hold data—**resilient distributed datasets** (**RDDs**), DataFrames, and Datasets.

RDDs

RDDs are an immutable and distributed collection of records partitioned across the worker nodes in a Spark cluster. They offer fault tolerance since, in the event of non-functional nodes or damaged partitions, RDD partitions can be recomputed, since all the dependency information needed to replicate each of its partitions is stored by the RDD itself. They also provide consistency, since each partition is immutable. RDDs are commonly used in Spark today in situations where you do not need to impose a schema when processing the data, such as when unstructured data is processed. Operations may be executed on RDDs via a low-level API that provides two broad categories of operation:

- **Transformations**: These are operations that return another RDD. Narrow transformations, for example, map operations, are operations that can be executed on arbitrary partitions of data without being dependent on other partitions. Wide transformations, for example, sorting, joining, and grouping, are operations that require the data to be repartitioned across the cluster. Certain transformations, such as sorting and grouping, require the data to be redistributed across partitions, a process known as *shuffling*. Because data needs to be redistributed, wide transformations requiring shuffling are expensive operations and should be minimized in Spark applications where possible.
- **Actions**: These are computational operations that return a value back to the driver, not another RDD. RDDs are said to be lazily evaluated, meaning that transformations are only computed when an action is called.

DataFrames

Like RDDs, they are an immutable and distributed collection of records partitioned across the worker nodes in a Spark cluster. However, unlike RDDs, data is organized into named columns conceptually similar to tables in relational databases and tabular data structures found in other programming languages, such as Python and R. Because DataFrames offer the ability to impose a schema on distributed data, they are more easily exposed to more familiar programming languages such as SQL, which makes them a popular and arguably easier data structure to work with and manipulate, as well as being more efficient than RDDs.

The main disadvantage of DataFrames however is that, similar to Spark SQL string queries, analysis errors are only caught at runtime and not during compilation. For example, imagine a DataFrame called df with the named columns firstname, lastname, and gender. Now imagine that we coded the following statement:

```
df.filter( df.age > 30 )
```

This statement attempts to filter the DataFrame based on a missing and unknown column called age. Using the DataFrame API, this error would not be caught at compile time but instead only at runtime, which could be costly and time-consuming if the Spark application in question involved multiple transformations and aggregations prior to this statement.

Datasets

Datasets extend DataFrames by providing type safety. This means that in the preceding example of the missing column, the Dataset API will throw a compile time error. In fact, DataFrames are actually an alias for Dataset[Row] where a Row is an untyped object that you may see in Spark applications written in Java. However, because R and Python have no compile-time type safety, this means that Datasets are not currently available to these languages.

There are numerous advantages to using the DataFrame and Dataset APIs over RDDs, including better performance and more efficient memory usage. The high-level APIs offered by DataFrame and Dataset also make it easier to perform standard operations such as filtering, grouping, and calculating statistical aggregations such as totals and averages. RDDs, however, are still useful because of the greater degree of control offered by its low-level API, including low-level transformations and actions. They also provide analysis errors at compile time and are well suited to unstructured data.

Jobs, stages, and tasks

Now that we know how Spark stores data during computational processing, let's return to its logical architecture to understand how Spark applications are logically broken down into smaller units for distributed processing.

Job

When an action is called in a Spark application, Spark will use a dependency graph to ascertain the datasets on which that action depends and thereafter formulate an execution plan. An execution plan is essentially a chain of datasets, beginning with the dataset furthest back all the way through to the final dataset, that are required to be computed in order to calculate the value to return to the driver program as a result of that action. This process is called a Spark job, with each job corresponding to one action.

Stage

If the Spark job and, hence, the action that resulted in the launching of that job, involves the shuffling of data (that is, the redistribution of data), then that job is broken down into stages. A new stage begins when network communication is required between the worker nodes. An individual stage is therefore defined as a collection of tasks processed by an individual executor with no dependency on other executors.

Tasks

Tasks are the smallest unit of execution in Spark, with a single task being executed on one executor; in other words, a single task cannot span multiple executors. All the tasks making up one stage share the same code to be executed, but act on different partitions of the data. The number of tasks that can be processed by an executor is bounded by the number of cores associated with that executor. Therefore, the total number of tasks that can be executed in parallel across an entire Spark cluster can be calculated by multiplying the number of cores per executor by the number of executors. This value then provides a quantifiable measure of the level of parallelism offered by your Spark cluster.

In Chapter 2, *Setting Up a Local Development Environment*, we will discuss how to install, configure, and administer a single-node standalone Spark cluster for development purposes, as well as discussing some of the basic configuration options exposed by Spark. Then, in Chapter 3, *Artificial Intelligence and Machine Learning*, and onward, we will take advantage of Spark's machine learning library, MLlib, so that we may employ Spark as a distributed advanced analytics engine. To learn more about Apache Spark, please visit http://spark.apache.org/.

Distributed messaging

Continuing our journey through distributed systems, the next category that we will discuss is distributed messaging systems. Typically, real-world IT systems are, in fact, a collection of distinct applications, potentially written in different languages using different underlying technologies and frameworks, that are integrated with one another. In order for messages to be sent between distinct applications, developers could potentially code the consumption logic into each individual application. This is a bad idea however—what happens if the type of message sent by an upstream application changes? In this case, the consumption logic would have to be rewritten, relevant applications updated, and the whole system retested.

Messaging systems, such as **Apache ActiveMQ** and **RabbitMQ**, overcome this problem by providing a middleman called a message broker. *Figure 1.10* illustrates how message brokers work at a high level:

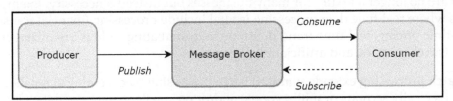

Figure 1.10: Message broker high-level overview

At a high level, **Producers** are applications that generate and send messages required for the functionality of the system. The **Message Broker** receives these messages and stores them inside queue data structures or buffers. **Consumer** applications, which are applications designed to process messages, subscribe to the message broker. The message broker then delivers these messages to the **Consumer** applications which consume and process them. Note that a single application can be a producer, consumer, or both.

Distributed messaging systems, which is one use case of **Apache Kafka**, extend traditional messaging systems by being able to partition and scale horizontally, while offering high throughput, high performance, fault tolerance, and replication, like many other distributed systems. This means that messages are never lost, while offering the ability to load balance requests and provide ordering guarantees. We will discuss Apache Kafka in more detail next, but in the context of a distributed streaming platform for real-time data.

Distributed streaming

Imagine processing the data stored in a traditional spreadsheet or text-based delimited files such as a CSV file. The type of processing that you will typically execute when using these types of data stores is referred to as **batch processing**. In batch processing, data is collated into some sort of group, in this case, the collection of lines in our spreadsheet or CSV file, and processed together as a group at some future time and date. Typically, these spreadsheets or CSV files will be refreshed with updated data at some juncture, at which point the same, or similar, processing will be undertaken, potentially all managed by some sort of schedule or timer. Traditionally, data processing systems would have been developed with batch processing in mind, including conventional data warehouses.

Today, however, batch processing alone is not enough. With the advent of the internet, social media, and more powerful technology, coupled with the demand for mass data consumption as soon as possible (ideally immediately), real-time data processing and analytics are no longer a luxury for many businesses but instead a necessity. Examples of use cases where real-time data processing is vital include processing financial transactions and real-time pricing, real-time fraud detection and combating serious organized crime, logistics, travel, robotics, and artificial intelligence.

Micro-batch processing extends standard batch processing by executing at smaller intervals (typically seconds or milliseconds) and/or on smaller batches of data. However, like batch processing, data is still processed a batch at a time.

Stream processing differs from micro-batch and batch processing in the fact that data processing is executed as and when individual data units arrive. Distributed streaming platforms, such as **Apache Kafka**, provide the ability to safely and securely move real-time data between systems and applications. Thereafter, distributed streaming engines, such as Apache Spark's Streaming library, **Spark Streaming**, and **Apache Storm**, allow us to process and analyze real-time data. In `Chapter 8`, *Real-Time Machine Learning Using Apache Spark*, we will discuss Spark Streaming in greater detail, where we will develop a real-time sentiment analysis model by combining Apache Kafka with Spark Streaming and Apache Spark's machine learning library, `MLlib`.

In the meantime, let's quickly take a look into how Apache Kafka works under the hood. Take a moment to think about what kind of things you would need to consider in order to engineer a real-time streaming platform:

- **Fault tolerance**: The platform must not lose real-time streams of data and have some way to store them in the event of partial system failure.
- **Ordering**: The platform must provide a means to guarantee that streams can be processed in the order that they are received, which is especially important to business applications where order is critical.

- **Reliability**: The platform must provide a means to reliably and efficiently move streams between various distinct applications and systems.

Apache Kafka provides all of these guarantees through its distributed streaming logical architecture, as illustrated in *Figure 1.11*:

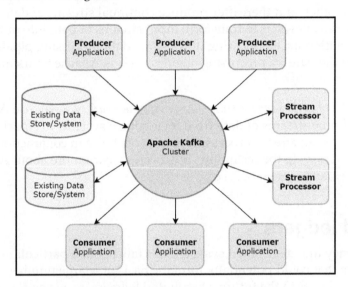

Figure 1.11: Apache Kafka logical architecture

In Apache Kafka, a *topic* refers to a stream of records belonging to a particular category. Kafka's Producer API allows producer applications to publish streams of records to one or more Kafka topics, and its Consumer API allows consumer applications to subscribe to one or more topics and thereafter receive and process the stream of records belonging to those topics. Topics in Kafka are said to be multi-subscriber, meaning that a single topic may have zero, one, or more consumers subscribed to it. Physically, a Kafka topic is stored as a sequence of ordered and immutable records that can only be appended to and are partitioned and replicated across the Kafka cluster, thereby providing scalability and fault tolerance for large systems. Kafka guarantees that producer messages are appended to a topic partition in the order that they are sent, with the producer application responsible for identifying which partition to assign records to, and that consumer applications can access records in the order in which they are persisted.

Kafka has become synonymous with real-time data because of its logical architecture and the guarantees that it provides when moving real-time streams of data between systems and applications. But Kafka can also be used as a stream processing engine as well in its own right via its Streams API, not just as a messaging system. By means of its Streams API, Kafka allows us to consume continual streams of data from input topics, process that data in some manner or other, and thereafter produce continual streams of data to output topics. In other words, Kafka allows us to transform input streams of data into output streams of data, thereby facilitating the engineering of real-time data processing pipelines in competition with other stream processing engines such as Apache Spark and Apache Storm.

In `Chapter 8`, *Real-Time Machine Learning Using Apache Spark*, we will use Apache Kafka to reliably move real-time streams of data from their source systems to Apache Spark. Apache Spark will then act as our stream processing engine of choice in conjunction with its machine learning library. In the meantime, however, to learn more about Apache Kafka, please visit `https://kafka.apache.org/`.

Distributed ledgers

To finish our journey into distributed systems, let's talk about a particular type of distributed system that could potentially form the basis of a large number of exciting cutting-edge technologies in the future. Distributed ledgers are a special class within distributed databases made famous recently by the prevalence of blockchain and subsequent cryptocurrencies such as Bitcoin.

Traditionally, when you make a purchase using your credit or debit card, the issuing bank acts as the centralized authority. As part of the transaction, a request is made to the bank to ascertain whether you have sufficient funds to complete the transaction. If you do, the bank keeps a record of the new transaction and deducts the amount from your balance, allowing you to complete the purchase. The bank keeps a record of this and all transactions on your account. If you ever wish to view your historic transactions and your current overall balance, you can access your account records online or via paper statements, all of which are managed by the trusted and central source—your bank.

Distributed ledgers, on the other hand, have no single trusted central authority. Instead, records are independently created and stored on separate nodes forming a distributed network, in other words, a distributed database, but data is never created nor passed through a central authority or master node. Every node in the distributed network processes every transaction. If you make a purchase using a cryptocurrency such as Bitcoin based on Blockchain technology, which is one form of distributed ledger, the nodes vote on the update. Once a majority consensus is reached, the distributed ledger is updated and the latest version of the ledger is saved on each node separately.

As described, Blockchain is one form of a distributed ledger. As well as sharing the fundamental features of distributed ledgers, in blockchain, data is grouped into blocks that are secured using cryptography. Records in blockchain cannot be altered or deleted once persisted, but can only be appended to, making blockchain particularly well suited to use cases where maintaining a secure historical view is important, such as financial transactions and cryptocurrencies including Bitcoin.

Artificial intelligence and machine learning

We have discussed how distributed systems can be employed to store, model, and process huge amounts of structured, semi-structured, and unstructured data, while providing horizontal scalability, fault tolerance, resilience, high availability, consistency, and high throughput. However, other fields of study have become prevalent today, seemingly in conjunction with the rise of big data—artificial intelligence and machine learning.

But why have these fields of study, the underlying mathematical theories of which have been around for decades, and even centuries in some cases, risen to prominence at the same time as big data? The answer to this question lies in understanding the benefits offered by this new breed of technology.

Distributed systems allow us to consolidate, aggregate, transform, process, and analyze vast volumes of previously disparate data. The process of consolidating these disparate datasets allows us to infer insights and uncover hidden relationships that would have been impossible previously. Furthermore, cluster computing, such as that offered by distributed systems, exposes more powerful and numerous hardware and software working together as a single logical unit that can be assigned to solve complex computational tasks such as those inherent to artificial intelligence and machine learning. Today, by combining these features, we can efficiently run advanced analytical algorithms to ultimately provide actionable insights, the level and breadth of which have never been seen before in many mainstream industries.

Apache Spark's machine learning library, `MLlib`, and `TensorFlow` are examples of libraries that have been developed to allow us to quickly and efficiently engineer and execute machine learning algorithms as part of analytical processing pipelines.

In `Chapter 3`, *Artificial Intelligence and Machine Learning*, we will discuss some of the high-level concepts behind common artificial intelligence and machine learning algorithms, as well as the logical architecture behind Apache Spark's machine learning library `MLlib`. Thereafter, in `Chapter 4`, *Supervised Learning Using Apache Spark*, through to `Chapter 8`, *Real-Time Machine Learning Using Apache Spark*, we will develop advanced analytical models with `MLlib` using real-world use cases, while exploring their underlying mathematical theory.

To learn more about `MLlib` and `TensorFlow`, please visit `https://spark.apache.org/mllib/` and `https://www.tensorflow.org/` respectively.

Cloud computing platforms

Traditionally, many large organizations have invested in expensive data centers to house their business-critical computing systems. These data centers are integrated with their corporate networks, allowing users to access both the data stored in these centers and increased processing capacity. One of the main advantages of large organizations maintaining their own data centers is that of security—both data and processing capacity is kept on-premise under their control and administration within largely closed networks.

However, with the advent of big data and more accessible artificial intelligence and machine learning-driven analytics, the need to store, model, process, and analyze huge volumes of data requiring scalable hardware, software, and potentially distributed clusters containing hundreds or thousands of physical or virtual nodes quickly makes maintaining your own 24/7 data centers less and less cost-effective.

Cloud computing platforms, such as **Amazon Web Services (AWS)**, **Microsoft Azure**, and the **Google Cloud Platform (GCP)**, provide a means to offload some or all of an organization's data storage, management, and processing requirements to remote platforms managed by technology companies and that are accessible over the internet. Today, these cloud computing platforms offer much more than just a place to remotely store an organization's ever-increasing data estate. They offer scalable storage, computational processing, administration, data governance, and security software services, as well as access to artificial intelligence and machine learning libraries and frameworks. These cloud computing platforms also tend to offer a **Pay-As-You-Go (PAYG)** pricing model, meaning that you only pay for the storage and processing capacity that you actually use, which can also be easily scaled up or down depending on requirements.

Organizations that are weary of storing their sensitive data on remote platforms accessible over the internet tend to instead architect and engineer hybrid systems, whereby sensitive data remains on-premise, but computational processing on anonymized or unattributable data is offloaded to the cloud, for example.

A well-architected and well-engineered system should provide a layer of abstraction between its infrastructure and its end users, including data analysts and data scientists—that is, the fact as to whether the data storage and processing infrastructure is on-premise or cloud-based should be invisible to these types of user. Furthermore, many of the distributed technologies and processing engines that we have discussed so far tend to be written in Java or C++, but expose their API or programming model to other language variants, such as Python, Scala, and R. This therefore makes them accessible to a wide range of end users, deployable on any machines that can run a JVM or compile C++ code. A significant number of cloud services offered by cloud computing platforms are, in fact, commercial service wrappers built around open source technologies guaranteeing availability and support. Therefore, once system administrators and end users become familiar with a particular class of technology, migrating to cloud computing platforms actually becomes a matter of configuration to optimize performance rather than learning an entirely new way to store, model, and process data. This is important, since a significant cost for many organizations is the training of its staff—if underlying technologies and frameworks can be reused as much as possible, then this is preferable to migrating to entirely new storage and processing paradigms.

Data insights platform

We have discussed the various systems, technologies, and frameworks available today to allow us to store, aggregate, manage, transform, process, and analyze vast volumes of structured, semi-structured, and unstructured data in both batch and real time in order to provide actionable insights and deliver real business value. We will conclude this chapter by discussing how all of these systems and technologies can fully integrate with one another to deliver a consolidated, high-performance, secure, and reliable data insights platform accessible to all parts of your organization.

Reference logical architecture

We can represent a data insights platform as a series of logical layers, where each layer provides a distinct functional capability. When we combine these layers, we form a reference logical architecture for a data insights platform, as illustrated in *Figure 1.12*:

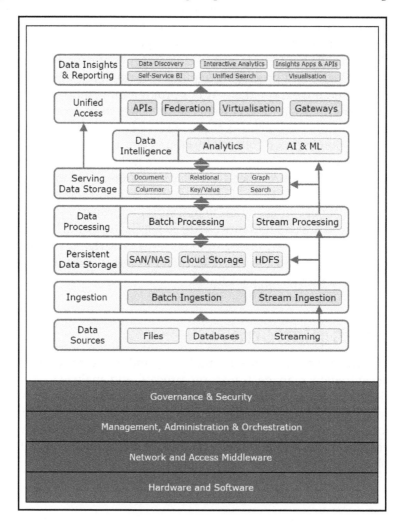

Figure 1.12: Data insights platform reference logical architecture

The logical layers in this data insights platform reference architecture are described in further detail in the following sub-sections.

Data sources layer

The data sources layer represents the various disparate data stores, datasets, and other source data systems that will provide the input data into the data insights platform. These disparate source data providers may contain either structured (for example, delimited text files, CSVs, and relational databases), semi-structured (for example, JSON and XML files) or unstructured (for example, images, videos, and audio) data.

Ingestion layer

The ingestion layer is responsible for consuming and thereafter moving the source data, no matter what their format and frequency, to either a persistent data store, or directly to a downstream data processing engine. The ingestion layer should be capable of supporting both batch data and stream-based event data. Examples of open source technologies used to implement the ingestion layer include the following:

- Apache Sqoop
- Apache Kafka
- Apache Flume

Persistent data storage layer

The persistent data storage layer is responsible for consuming and persisting the raw source data provided by the ingestion layer. Little or no transformation of the raw source data takes place before it is persisted to ensure that the raw data remains in its original format. A data lake is a class of persistent data store that is often implemented to store raw data in this manner. Example technologies used to implement the persistent data storage layer include the following:

- Traditional network-based stores, such as **Storage Area Networks** (**SAN**) and **Network Attached Storage** (**NAS**)
- Open source technologies, such as the HDFS
- Cloud-based technologies, such as **AWS S3** and **Azure BLOBs**

Data processing layer

The data processing layer is responsible for the transformation, enrichment, and validation of the raw data gathered from either the persistent data store or directly from the ingestion layer. The data processing layer models the data according to downstream business and analytical requirements and prepares it for either persistence in the serving data storage layer, or for processing by data intelligence applications. Again, the data processing layer must be capable of processing both batch data and stream-based event data. Examples of open source technologies used to implement the data processing layer include the following:

- Apache Hive
- Apache Spark, including Spark Streaming (DStreams) and Structured Streaming
- Apache Kafka
- Apache Storm

Serving data storage layer

The serving analytical data storage layer is responsible for persisting the transformed, enriched, and validated data produced by the data processing layer in data stores that maintain the data model structures so that they are ready to serve downstream data intelligence and data insight applications. This minimizes or removes the need for further data transformations since the data is already persisted in highly-optimized data structures relevant to the type of processing required. The types of data stores provisioned in the serving analytical data storage layer are dependent on business and analytical requirements, and may include any, or a combination of, the following (stated along with examples of open source implementations):

- Relational databases, such as **PostgreSQL** and **MySQL**
- Document databases, such as **Apache CouchDB** and **MongoDB**
- Columnar databases, such as **Apache Cassandra** and **Apache HBase**
- Key-value databases, such as **Redis** and **Voldemort**
- Graph databases and frameworks, such as **Apache TinkerPop**
- Search engines, such as **Apache Lucene** and **Elasticsearch**

Data intelligence layer

The data intelligence layer is responsible for executing advanced analytical pipelines, both predictive and prescriptive, on both the transformed batch data and stream-based event data. Advanced analytical pipelines may include artificial intelligence services such as image and speech analysis, cognitive computing, and complex reasoning, as well as machine learning models and natural language processing. Examples of open source, advanced analytical libraries and frameworks used to implement the data intelligence layer include the following:

- **Apache Spark MLlib** (API accessible via Python, R, Java, and Scala)
- **TensorFlow** (API accessible via Python, Java, C++, Go, and JavaScript, with third-party bindings available in C#, R, Haskell, Ruby, and Scala)

Unified access layer

The unified access layer is responsible for providing access to both the serving analytical data storage layer and third-party APIs exposed by the data intelligence layer. The unified access layer should provide universal, scalable, and secure access to any downstream applications and systems that require it, and typically involves the architecting and engineering of APIs and/or implementations of data federation and virtualization patterns. Examples of open source technologies used to implement the unified access layer include the following:

- Spring framework
- Apache Drill

Data insights and reporting layer

The data insights and reporting layer is responsible for exposing the data insights platform to end users, including data analysts and data scientists. Data discovery, self-service business intelligence, search, visualization, data insights, and interactive analytical applications can all be provisioned in this layer and can access both the transformed data in the serving analytical data storage layer and third-party APIs in the data intelligence layer, all via the unified access layer. The fundamental purpose of the data insights and reporting layer is to deliver actionable insights and business value derived from all the structured, semi-structured, and unstructured data available to the data insights platform in both batch and real time. Examples of open source technologies used to implement the data insights and reporting layer that are also accessible to end users include the following:

- Apache Zeppelin
- Jupyter Notebook

- Elastic Kibana
- BIRT Reporting
- Custom JavaScript-based web applications for search and visualization

Examples of commercial technologies include the following business intelligence applications for creating dashboards and reporting:

- Tableau
- Microsoft Power BI
- SAP Lumira
- QlikView

Platform governance, management, and administration

Finally, since the data insights platform is designed to be accessible by all areas of an organization, and will store sensitive data leading to the generation of actionable insights, the systems it contains must be properly governed, managed, and administered. Therefore, the following additional logical layers are required in order to provision a secure enterprise and production-grade platform:

- **Governance and Security**: This layer includes **identity and access management (IDAM)** and data governance tooling. Open source technologies used to implement this layer include the following:
    - Apache Knox (Hadoop Authentication Gateway)
    - Apache Metron (Security Analytics Framework)
    - Apache Ranger (Monitor Data Security)
    - OpenLDAP (Lightweight Directory Access Protocol Implementation)
- **Management, Administration, and Orchestration**: This layer includes DevOps processes (such as version control, automated builds, and deployment), cluster monitoring and administration software, and scheduling and workflow management tooling. Open source technologies used to implement this layer include the following:
    - Jenkins (Automation Server)
    - Git (Version Control)
    - Apache Ambari (Administration, Monitoring, and Management)
    - Apache Oozie (Workflow Scheduling)

- **Network and Access Middleware**: This layer handles network connectivity and communication, and includes network security, monitoring, and intrusion detection software.
- **Hardware and Software**: This layer contains the physical storage, compute, and network infrastructure on which the data insights platform is deployed. The physical components may be on-premise, cloud-based, or a hybrid combination of the two.

Open source implementation

Figure 1.13 illustrates an example implementation of the reference data insights platform using only open source technologies and frameworks:

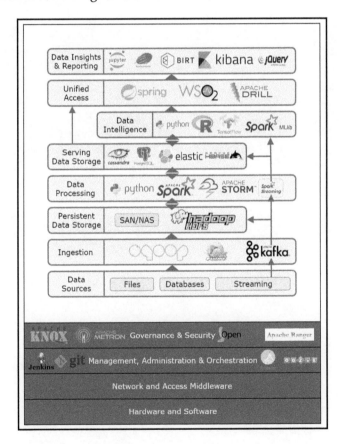

Figure 1.13: Example of open source implementation of the data insights platform

Summary

In this chapter, we have explored a new breed of distributed and scalable technologies that allow us to reliably and securely store, manage, model, transform, process, and analyze huge volumes of structured, semi-structured, and unstructured data in both batch and real time in order to derive real actionable insights using advanced analytics.

In the next chapter, we will guide you through how to install, configure, deploy, and administer a single-node analytical development environment utilizing a subset of these technologies, including Apache Spark, Apache Kafka, Jupyter Notebook, Python, Java, and Scala!

2
Setting Up a Local Development Environment

In this chapter, we will install, configure, and deploy a local analytical development environment by provisioning a self-contained single-node cluster that will allow us to do the following:

- Prototype and develop machine learning models and pipelines in Python
- Demonstrate the functionality and usage of Apache Spark's machine learning library, `MLlib`, via the Spark Python API (PySpark)
- Develop and test machine learning models on a single-node cluster using small sample datasets, and thereafter scale up to multi-node clusters processing much larger datasets with little or no code changes required

Our single-node cluster will host the following technologies:

- **Operating system**: CentOS Linux 7
  `https://www.centos.org/download/`
- **General Purpose Programming Languages**:
  - Java SE Development Kit (JDK) 8 (8u181)
    `https://www.oracle.com/technetwork/java/javase/downloads/index.html`
  - Scala 2.11.x (2.11.12)
    `https://www.scala-lang.org/download/all.html`
  - Python 3.x (3.6) via Anaconda 5.x (5.2) Python Distribution
    `https://www.anaconda.com/download/`
- **General purpose distributed processing engine**: Apache Spark 2.3.x (2.3.2)
  `http://spark.apache.org/downloads.html`
- **Distributed streaming platform**: Apache Kafka 2 (2.0.0)
  `https://kafka.apache.org/downloads`

CentOS Linux 7 virtual machine

First of all, we will assume that you have access to a physical or virtual machine provisioned with the CentOS 7 operating system. CentOS 7 is a free Linux distribution derived from **Red Hat Enterprise Linux** (**RHEL**). It is commonly used, along with its licensed upstream parent, RHEL, as the operating system of choice for Linux-based servers, since it is stable and backed by a large active community with detailed documentation. All the commands that we will use to install the various technologies listed previously will be Linux shell commands to be executed on a single CentOS 7 (or RHEL) machine, whether physical or virtual. If you do not have access to a CentOS 7 machine, then there are quite a few options available to provision a CentOS 7 virtual machine:

- Cloud computing platforms such as **Amazon Web Services** (**AWS**), **Microsoft Azure**, and the **Google Cloud Platform** (**GCP**) all allow you to stand up virtual machines using a **Pay-As-You-Go** (**PAYG**) pricing model. Often, the major cloud computing platforms also provide a free tier for new users with a small amount of free capacity in order to trial their services. To learn more about these major cloud computing platforms, please visit the following websites:
  - AWS: https://aws.amazon.com/
  - Microsoft Azure: https://azure.microsoft.com
  - GCP: https://cloud.google.com/

- **Virtual Private Server** (**VPS**) hosting companies, such as **Linode** and **Digital Ocean**, also provide the ability to provision low-cost CentOS virtual machines. These VPS providers often employ a much simpler pricing model consisting only of virtual machines of various specifications. To learn more about these major VPS providers, please visit the following websites:
  - Linode: https://www.linode.com/
  - Digital Ocean: https://www.digitalocean.com/

- A common and free option, particularly for local development environments used for prototyping and testing, is to provision your own virtual machine hosted by your personal physical desktop or laptop. Virtualization software such as **Oracle VirtualBox** (open source) and **VMWare Workstation Player** (free for personal use) allow you to set up and run virtual machines on your own personal physical devices. To learn more about these virtualization software services, please visit the following websites:
  - Oracle VirtualBox: https://www.virtualbox.org/
  - VMWare Workstation Player: https://www.vmware.com/

For the remainder of this chapter, we will assume that you have provisioned a 64-bit CentOS 7 machine and that you have either direct desktop access to it, or network access to it via both HTTP and SSH protocols. Though the specifications of your virtual machine may differ, we would recommend the following minimum virtual hardware requirements in order to efficiently run the examples in the remainder of this book:

- Operating System: CentOS 7 (minimum installation)
- Virtual CPUs: 4
- Memory: 8 GB
- Storage: 20 GB

In our case, our virtual machine has the following network properties and will be referenced hereafter as such. These will be different for your virtual machine:

- Static IP address: `192.168.56.10`
- Netmask: `255.255.255.0`
- **Fully qualified domain name** (**FQDN**): `packt.dev.keisan.io`

 Note that the security of your virtual machine, and the subsequent software services that it hosts, including big data technologies, is beyond the scope of this book. Should you wish to learn more about how to harden your base operating system and common software services in order to protect against external attacks, we recommend visiting `https://www.cisecurity.org/cis-benchmarks/` as well as the individual software service websites themselves, such as `https://spark.apache.org/docs/latest/security.html` for Apache Spark security.

Java SE Development Kit 8

Java is a general purpose programming language often used for **object-oriented programming** (**OOP**). Many of the distributed technologies that we discussed in Chapter 1, *The Big Data Ecosystem*, are originally written in Java. As such, the **Java Development Kit** (**JDK**) is required to be installed in our local development environment in order to run those software services within **Java Virtual Machines** (**JVM**). Apache Spark 2.3.x requires Java 8+ in order to run. To install Oracle Java SE Development Kit 8, please execute the following shell commands as the Linux *root* user or another user with elevated privileges:

```
> rpm -ivh jdk-8u181-linux-x64.rpm
> vi /etc/profile.d/java.sh

    $ export PATH=/usr/java/default/bin:$PATH
```

```
$ export JAVA_HOME=/usr/java/default
```

```
> source /etc/profile.d/java.sh
> echo $PATH
> echo $JAVA_HOME
```

These commands will install JDK 8 and, thereafter, add the location of the Java binaries to the global PATH variable, allowing any local Linux user to run Java-based programs. To check that Java 8 has been installed successfully, the following command should return the version of Java installed, demonstrated as follows:

```
> java -version
    $ java version "1.8.0_181"
    $ Java(TM) SE Runtime Environment (build 1.8.0_181-b13)
    $ Java HotSpot(TM) 64-Bit Server VM (build 25.181-b13, mixed mode)
```

Scala 2.11

Scala is a general purpose programming language used for both object-oriented programming and functional programming. Apache Spark is, in fact, written in the Scala programming language. However, as described in Chapter 1, *The Big Data Ecosystem*, Spark applications can be written in a variety of languages, including Java, Scala, Python, and R. Though the pros and cons of Scala versus Python is beyond the scope of this book, Scala is generally faster than Python within the context of data analysis and naturally more tightly integrated with Spark. Python, however, currently offers a more comprehensive library of advanced third-party data science tools and frameworks and is arguably easier to learn and use. The code examples provided for this book have been written in Python 3. However, this sub-section describes the steps required in order to install Scala should you wish to develop Scala-based applications.

Referring to Scala specifically, Apache Spark 2.3.2 requires Scala 2.11.x in order to run Scala-based Spark applications. In order to install Scala 2.11.12, please execute the following shell commands as the Linux root user or another user with elevated privileges:

```
> rpm -ivh scala-2.11.12.rpm
```

These commands will install Scala 2.11.12 and place its binaries in a globally accessible location, allowing any local Linux user to run Scala applications, whether Spark-based or not. To check that Scala 2.11.12 has been installed successfully, the following command should return the version of Scala installed:

```
> scala -version
    $ Scala code runner version 2.11.12
```

You can also access the Scala shell and execute interactive Scala commands as follows:

```
> scala
>> 1+2
     $ res0: Int = 3
>> :q
```

Anaconda 5 with Python 3

Anaconda is a distribution of the Python general purpose programming language. Not only does it contain the Python interpreter, but it also comes bundled with a wide range of commonly used Python data science packages out of the box and a Python package management system called **conda**, making it quick and easy to provision a Python-based data science platform. In fact, we will be taking advantage of some of the pre-bundled Python packages in later chapters.

Anaconda 5.2 comes bundled with Python 3.6. Apache Spark 2.3.x supports both branches of Python, namely Python 2 and Python 3. Specifically, it supports Python 2.7+ and Python 3.4+. As described earlier, the code examples provided for this book have been written in Python 3.

In order to install Anaconda 5.2, please execute the following shell commands. You may or may not choose to execute these shell commands as the Linux root user. If you do not, Anaconda will be installed for the local Linux user running these commands and does not require administrator privileges:

```
> bash Anaconda3-5.2.0-Linux-x86_64.sh
> Do you accept the license terms? [yes|no]
>>> yes
> Do you wish the installer to prepend the Anaconda3 install location to
PATH in your .bashrc ? [yes|no]
>>> yes
  The last command will add the location of the Anaconda, and hence Python,
binaries to your local PATH variable, allowing your local Linux user to run
both Python-based programs (overriding any existing Python interpreters
already installed on the operating system) and conda commands. Note that
you may need to open a new Linux shell in order for the local PATH updates
to take effect.
```

To check that Anaconda 5.2 and, hence, Python 3.6 have been installed successfully, the following command should return the version of conda installed:

```
> conda --version
     $ conda 4.5.4
```

You can also access the Python shell and execute interactive Python commands as follows:

```
> python
      $ Python 3.6.5 | Anaconda, Inc.
>>> import sys
>>> sys.path
>>> quit()
```

Basic conda commands

In this sub-section, we will provide some basic conda commands for your reference. These commands assume that your virtual machine can access either the internet or a local Python repository.

In order to upgrade the version of conda and/or Anaconda as a whole, you can execute the following commands:

```
> conda update conda
> conda update anaconda
```

To install or update individual Python packages, you can execute the following commands:

```
> conda install <name of Python package>
> conda update <name of Python package>
```

Finally, in order to list the current Python packages and versions installed in your Anaconda distribution, you can execute the following command:

```
> conda list
```

To learn more about the conda package management system, please visit `https://conda.io/docs/index.html`.

Additional Python packages

The following Python packages, which are not already contained within the default Anaconda distribution, are required for our local development environment. Please execute the following shell commands to install these prerequisite Python packages:

```
> conda install -c conda-forge findspark
> conda install -c conda-forge pykafka
> conda install -c conda-forge tweepy
> conda install -c conda-forge tensorflow
> conda install -c conda-forge keras
```

Jupyter Notebook

Jupyter Notebook is an open source, web-based application designed for *interactive* analytics that comes bundled with the Anaconda distribution. Since it is designed for interactive analytics, it is best suited for ad hoc queries, live simulations, prototyping, and a means to visualize your data and to look for any trends and patterns prior to developing production-ready data science models. **Apache Zeppelin** is another example of an open source, web-based notebook used for similar purposes. Notebooks such as Jupyter Notebook and Apache Zeppelin tend to support multiple kernels, meaning that you can use various general purpose programming languages including Python and Scala.

One of the core advantages of notebooks is that they persist both your input code and any output data structures and visualizations that your code generates, including graphs, charts, and tables. However, they are *not* fully-fledged **integrated development environments** (IDE). This means that, in general, they should not be used for the development of code intended for production-grade data engineering or analytical pipelines. This is because they are difficult (but not impossible) to manage in version control systems such as Git, as they persist both input code and intermediate output structures. As such, they are also difficult to build code artifacts from and to deploy automatically using typical DevOps pipelines. Therefore, notebooks remain ideally suited for interactive analytics, ad hoc queries, and for prototyping.

The majority of the code files provided for this book are, in fact, Jupyter Notebook files (`.ipynb`), using the Python 3 kernel, so that readers may see the output of our models immediately. Should you, in the future, wish to write data science code that will eventually be deployed to production-grade systems, we strongly recommend writing your code in a proper IDE such as the following:

- Eclipse: `https://www.eclipse.org/ide/`
- IntelliJ IDEA: `https://www.jetbrains.com/idea/`
- PyCharm: `https://www.jetbrains.com/pycharm/`
- Microsoft **Visual Studio Code** (**VS Code**): `https://code.visualstudio.com/`

As mentioned earlier, Jupyter Notebook is already bundled with the Anaconda distribution. However, a few configuration steps are recommended in order to access it. Please execute the following shell commands as your local Linux user in order to generate a per-user Jupyter Notebook configuration file that you can then edit based on per-user preferences:

```
> jupyter notebook --generate-config
      $ Writing default config to:
/home/packt/.jupyter/jupyter_notebook_config.py
> vi /home/packt/.jupyter/jupyter_notebook_config.py
      Line 174: c.NotebookApp.ip = '192.168.56.10'
      Line 214: c.NotebookApp.notebook_dir =
'/data/workspaces/packt/jupyter/notebooks/'
      Line 240: c.NotebookApp.port = 8888
```

These commands will configure a per-user Jupyter Notebook instance to listen on a dedicated IP address (in our case, `192.168.56.10`) using a designated port (in our case `8888`), and to work from a pre-defined base directory in which to persist Jupyter Notebook code files (in our case `/data/workspaces/packt/jupyter/notebooks`). Note that you should amend these properties based on your specific environment.

Starting Jupyter Notebook

If you have desktop-based access to your CentOS virtual machine, the easiest way to instantiate a new per-user Jupyter Notebook instance is to execute the following shell command as your local Linux user:

```
> jupyter notebook
```

However, should you only have SSH or command-line access with no GUI, then you should use the following command instead:

```
> jupyter notebook --no-browser
```

The latter command will stop Jupyter from automatically opening a local browser session. In either case, the resultant logs will state the full URL (including the security token by default) that can be used to access your instance of Jupyter Notebook. The URL should look similar to the following:

```
http://192.168.56.10:8888/?token=6ebb5f6a321b478162802a97b8e463a1a053df
12fcf9d99c
```

Please copy and paste this URL into an internet browser supported by Jupyter Notebook (Google Chrome, Mozilla Firefox, or Apple Safari). If successful, a screen similar to the screenshot illustrated in *Figure 2.1* should be returned:

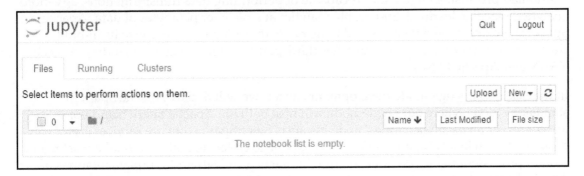

Figure 2.1: Jupyter Notebook web session

Troubleshooting Jupyter Notebook

Since Jupyter Notebook is a web-based application, it is accessible via the HTTP protocol at the designated port number. If you are accessing the generated URL via a remote internet browser and it cannot connect, then please check your firewall settings (and SELinux in the case of CentOS and RHEL) on your virtual machine to ensure that access to the designated port number is provisioned from your location. For example, the following shell commands executed by the Linux *root* user, or another user with elevated privileges, will open port 8888 in the CentOS 7 firewall via its public zone:

```
> firewall-cmd --get-active-zones
> firewall-cmd --zone=public --add-port=8888/tcp --permanent
> firewall-cmd --reload
> firewall-cmd --list-all
```

Please contact your system administrator or refer to your cloud platform documentation for further network-related information and troubleshooting.

To learn more about Jupyter Notebook, its configuration, and common troubleshooting, please visit https://jupyter-notebook.readthedocs.io/en/stable/index.html.

Apache Spark 2.3

As described in Chapter 1, *The Big Data Ecosystem*, Apache Spark is a general purpose distributed processing engine that is capable of performing data transformations, advanced analytics, machine learning, and graph analytics at scale over petabytes of data. Apache Spark can be deployed either in standalone mode (meaning that we utilize its in-built cluster manager) or integrated with other third-party cluster managers including Apache YARN and Apache Mesos.

In the case of our single-node development cluster, we will deploy Apache Spark in standalone mode where our single-node will host both the Apache Spark Standalone Master server and a single worker node instance. Since Spark software services are designed to run in a JVM, it is perfectly acceptable to co-locate both standalone master and worker processes on a single node, though in practice, in real-world implementations of Apache Spark, clusters can be much larger with multiple worker nodes provisioned. Our single-node Apache Spark cluster will still allow us to prototype and develop Spark applications and machine learning models that can still take advantage of the parallelism offered by a multi-core single machine, and thereafter are capable of being deployed to larger clusters and datasets with ease.

Also note that we will be installing Apache Spark 2.3.2 direct from its pre-built binaries available on the official Apache Spark website at http://spark.apache.org/downloads. html. Nowadays, it is common for distributed technologies such as Spark, Kafka, and Hadoop components to be installed together at the same time via consolidated big data platforms such as those offered by **Hortonworks Data Platform** (**HDP**), **Cloudera**, and **MapR**. The benefits of using consolidated platforms such as these include the deployment of individual component versions that have been fully tested together and guaranteed to fully integrate with one another, as well as web-based installation, monitoring, administration, and support.

Spark binaries

Please execute the following shell commands as a local Linux user to extract the Apache Spark binaries. In our case, we will be installing the Spark binaries into /opt:

```
> tar -xzf spark-2.3.2-bin-hadoop2.7.tgz -C /opt
```

The resultant Spark parent directory will have the following structure:

- `bin`: Shell scripts for local Spark services, such as `spark-submit`
- `sbin`: Shell scripts, including starting and stopping Spark services
- `conf`: Spark configuration files
- `jars`: Spark library dependencies
- `python`: Spark's Python API, called PySpark
- `R`: Spark's R API, called SparkR

Local working directories

Each node in a Spark cluster (in our case, just the single node) will generate log files as well as local working files, such as when shuffling and serializing RDD data. The following commands will create defined local directories in which to store these local working outputs, the paths of which you can edit as per your preferences and which will be used in later configuration files:

```
> mkdir -p /data/spark/local/data
> mkdir -p /data/spark/local/logs
> mkdir -p /data/spark/local/pid
> mkdir -p /data/spark/local/worker
```

Spark configuration

Configuration can be applied to Spark in the following ways:

- **Spark properties** control application-level settings, including execution behavior, memory management, dynamic allocation, scheduling, and security, which can be defined in the following order of precedence:
  - Via a Spark configuration programmatic object called `SparkConf` defined in your driver program
  - Via command-line arguments passed to `spark-submit` or `spark-shell`
  - Via default options set in `conf/spark-defaults.conf`
- **Environmental variables** control per-machine settings, such as the local IP address of the local worker node, and which can be defined in `conf/spark-env.sh`.

Spark properties

In our case, we will set some basic default Spark properties via `conf/spark-defaults.conf`, freeing us to concentrate on the data science content in future chapters. This can be achieved by executing the following shell commands (edit the values as per your environment):

```
> cp conf/spark-defaults.conf.template conf/spark-defaults.conf
> vi conf/spark-defaults.conf
        $ spark.master spark://192.168.56.10:7077
        $ spark.driver.cores 1
        $ spark.driver.maxResultSize 0
        $ spark.driver.memory 2g
        $ spark.executor.memory 2g
        $ spark.executor.cores 2
        $ spark.serializer org.apache.spark.serializer.KryoSerializer
        $ spark.rdd.compress true
        $ spark.kryoserializer.buffer.max 128m
```

Environmental variables

We will also set basic environmental variables via `conf/spark-env.sh` as follows (edit the values as per your environment):

```
> cp conf/spark-env.sh.template conf/spark-env.sh
> vi conf/spark-env.sh
        $ export SPARK_LOCAL_IP=192.168.56.10
        $ export SPARK_LOCAL_DIRS=/data/spark/local/data
        $ export SPARK_MASTER_HOST=192.168.56.10
        $ export SPARK_WORKER_DIR=/data/spark/local/worker
        $ export SPARK_CONF_DIR=/opt/spark-2.3.2-bin-hadoop2.7/conf
        $ export SPARK_LOG_DIR=/data/spark/local/logs
        $ export SPARK_PID_DIR=/data/spark/local/pid
```

To learn more about the various Spark configuration options available, including an exhaustive list of Spark properties and environmental variables, please visit `https://spark.apache.org/docs/latest/configuration.html`.

Standalone master server

We are now ready to start the Spark standalone master server, as follows:

```
> sbin/start-master.sh
```

To check whether this was successful, you can examine the Spark logs as written to SPARK_LOG_DIR. Spark applications can be submitted to the standalone master server at spark://<Master IP Address>:7077 (port 7077 by default) or spark://<Master IP Address>:6066 using its REST URL in cluster mode (port 6066 by default).

The Spark Master server also provides an out-of-the-box master web **User Interface** (**UI**) in which running Spark applications and workers can be monitored and performance diagnosed. By default, this master web UI is accessible via HTTP on port 8080, in other words, http://<Master IP Address>:8080, the interface of which is illustrated in *Figure 2.2*:

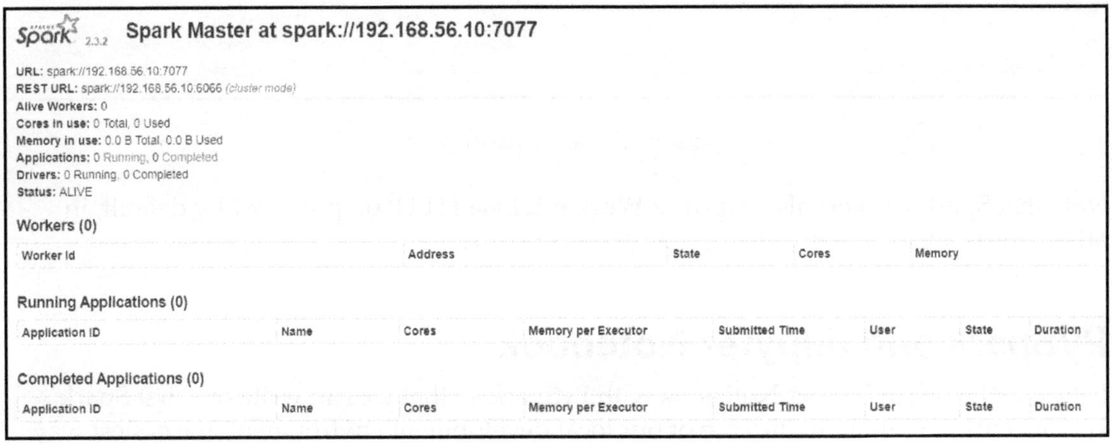

Spark 2.3.2 **Spark Master at spark://192.168.56.10:7077**

URL: spark://192.168.56.10:7077
REST URL: spark://192.168.56.10:6066 *(cluster mode)*
Alive Workers: 0
Cores in use: 0 Total, 0 Used
Memory in use: 0.0 B Total, 0.0 B Used
Applications: 0 Running, 0 Completed
Drivers: 0 Running, 0 Completed
Status: ALIVE

Workers (0)

Worker Id		Address		State	Cores	Memory	

Running Applications (0)

Application ID	Name	Cores	Memory per Executor	Submitted Time	User	State	Duration

Completed Applications (0)

Application ID	Name	Cores	Memory per Executor	Submitted Time	User	State	Duration

Figure 2.2: Spark standalone master server web UI

Again, in the event that you cannot access this URL via a remote internet browser, you may need to open up port 8080 (by default) in your firewall and/or SELinux settings.

Spark worker node

We are now ready to start our Spark Worker node, as follows:

```
> sbin/start-slave.sh spark://192.168.56.10:7077
```

Again, to check whether this was successful, you can examine the Spark logs as written to `SPARK_LOG_DIR`. You can also access the Spark Master web UI to confirm that the worker has been registered successfully, as illustrated in *Figure 2.3*:

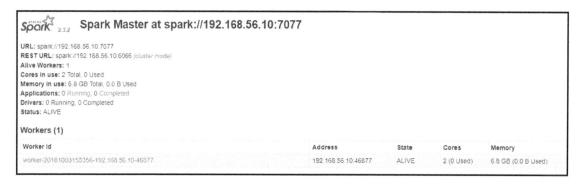

Figure 2.3: Spark worker successfully registered

Note that Spark workers also expose a **Worker UI** via HTTP on port 8081 by default, in other words, `http://<Worker IP Address>:8081`.

PySpark and Jupyter Notebook

Let's now integrate Jupyter Notebook with PySpark so that we can write our first Spark applications in Python! In the case of our local development environment, the easiest way to integrate Jupyter Notebook with PySpark is to set a global `SPARK_HOME` environmental variable that points to the directory containing the Spark binaries. Thereafter, we can employ the `findspark` Python package, as installed earlier, that will append the location of `SPARK_HOME`, and hence the PySpark API, to `sys.path` at runtime. Note that `findspark` should not be used for production-grade code development—instead, Spark applications should be deployed as code artifacts submitted via `spark-submit`.

Please execute the following shell commands as the Linux root user, or another user with elevated privileges, in order to define a global environmental variable called SPARK_HOME (or, alternatively, add it to your local Linux user's .bashrc file, which requires no administrative privileges):

```
> cd /etc/profile.d
> vi spark.sh
      $ export SPARK_HOME=/opt/spark-2.3.2-bin-hadoop2.7
> source spark.sh
```

 You will need to restart any running Jupyter Notebook instances, and the underlying Terminal sessions from which they were spawned, in order for the SPARK_HOME environmental variable to be successfully recognized and registered by findspark.

We are now ready to write our first Spark application in Python! Instantiate a Jupyter Notebook instance, access it via your internet browser, and create a new Python 3 notebook containing the following code (it may be easier to split the following code over separate notebook cells for future ease of reference):

```python
# (1) Import required Python dependencies
import findspark
findspark.init()
from pyspark import SparkContext, SparkConf
import random

# (2) Instantiate the Spark Context
conf = SparkConf()
   .setMaster("spark://192.168.56.10:7077")
   .setAppName("Calculate Pi")
sc = SparkContext(conf=conf)

# (3) Calculate the value of Pi i.e. 3.14...
def inside(p):
    x, y = random.random(), random.random()
    return x*x + y*y < 1

num_samples = 100
count = sc.parallelize(range(0, num_samples)).filter(inside).count()
pi = 4 * count / num_samples

# (4) Print the value of Pi
print(pi)

# (5) Stop the Spark Context
sc.stop()
```

This PySpark application, at a high level, works as follows:

1. Import the required Python dependencies, including `findspark` and `pyspark`
2. Create a Spark context, which tells the Spark application how to connect to the Spark cluster, by instantiating it with a `SparkConf` object that provides application-level settings at a higher level of precedence
3. Calculate the mathematical value of Pi π
4. Print the value of Pi and display it in Jupyter Notebook as a cell output
5. Stop the Spark context that terminates the Spark application

If you access the Spark Master web UI before executing `sc.stop()`, the Spark application will be listed under **Running Applications**, at which time you may view its underlying worker and executor log files. If you access the Spark Master web UI following execution of `sc.stop()`, the Spark application will be listed under **Completed Applications**.

Note that this notebook can be downloaded from the GitHub repository accompanying this book and is called `chp02-test-jupyter-notebook-with-pyspark.ipynb`.

Apache Kafka 2.0

To finish off our local development environment, we will install Apache Kafka. As described in `Chapter 1`, *The Big Data Ecosystem*, Apache Kafka is a distributed streaming platform. We will use Apache Kafka in `Chapter 8`, *Real-Time Machine Learning Using Apache Spark*, to develop a real-time analytical model by combining it with Spark Streaming and `MLlib`.

Again, for the purposes of our single-node development cluster, Apache Kafka will be deployed on the same single node as the Apache Spark software services. We will also be installing the version of Apache Kafka 2.0.0 that has been built for Scala 2.11.

Kafka binaries

After downloading the Kafka release, the first thing we need to do is to extract and install the pre-compiled binaries on our single-node cluster. In our case, we will be installing the Kafka binaries into /opt. Please execute the following shell commands as a local Linux user to extract the Apache Kafka binaries:

```
> tar -xzf kafka_2.11-2.0.0.tgz -C /opt
> cd /opt/kafka_2.11-2.0.0
```

Local working directories

As with Apache Spark processes, Apache Kafka processes also require their own local working directories to persist local data and log files. The following commands will create defined local directories in which to store these local working outputs, the paths of which you can edit as per your preferences:

```
> mkdir -p /data/zookeeper/local/data
> mkdir -p /data/kafka/local/logs
```

Kafka configuration

We will also set some basic configuration as follows (edit the values as per your environment):

```
> vi config/zookeeper.properties
    $ dataDir=/data/zookeeper/local/data
> vi config/server.properties
    $ listeners=PLAINTEXT://192.168.56.10:9092
    $ log.dirs=/data/kafka/local/logs
    $ zookeeper.connect=192.168.56.10:2181
```

Start the Kafka server

We are now ready to start Apache Kafka as follows:

```
> bin/zookeeper-server-start.sh -daemon config/zookeeper.properties
> bin/kafka-server-start.sh -daemon config/server.properties
```

Testing Kafka

Finally, we can test our Kafka installation by creating a test topic as follows:

```
> bin/kafka-topics.sh --create --zookeeper 192.168.56.10:2181 --
replication-factor 1 --partitions 1 --topic our-first-topic
    $ Created topic "our-first-topic".
> bin/kafka-topics.sh --list --zookeeper 192.168.56.10:2181
    $ our-first-topic
```

Once we have created our test topic, let's start a command-line producer application and send some test messages to this topic as follows:

```
> bin/kafka-console-producer.sh --broker-list 192.168.56.10:9092 --topic
our-first-topic
 > This is my 1st test message
 > This is my 2nd test message
 > This is my 3rd test message
```

Finally, let's start a command-line consumer application (in another Terminal session) to consume these test messages and print them to the console, as follows:

```
> bin/kafka-console-consumer.sh --bootstrap-server 192.168.56.10:9092 --
topic our-first-topic --from-beginning
    $ This is my 1st test message
    $ This is my 2nd test message
    $ This is my 3rd test message
```

In fact, if you keep typing new messages in the Terminal running the producer application, you will see them immediately being consumed by the consumer application and printed to the console in its Terminal!

Summary

In this chapter, we have installed, configured, and deployed a local analytical development environment consisting of a single-node Apache Spark 2.3.2 and Apache Kafka 2.0.0 cluster that will also allow us to interactively develop Spark applications using Python 3.6 via Jupyter Notebook.

In the next chapter, we will discuss some of the high-level concepts behind common artificial intelligence and machine learning algorithms, as well as introducing Apache Spark's machine learning library, MLlib!

Artificial Intelligence and Machine Learning

3

In this chapter, we will define what we mean by artificial intelligence, machine learning, and cognitive computing. We will study common classes of algorithms within the field of machine learning and its broader applications, including the following:

- Supervised learning
- Unsupervised learning
- Reinforced learning
- Deep learning
- Natural language processing
- Cognitive computing
- Apache Spark's machine learning library, `MLlib`, and how it can be used to implement these algorithms within machine learning pipelines

Artificial intelligence

Artificial intelligence is a broad term given to the theory and application of machines that exhibit intelligent behavior. Artificial intelligence encompasses many applied fields of study, including machine learning and subsequent deep learning, as illustrated in *Figure 3.1*:

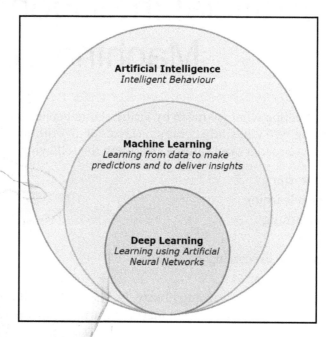

Figure 3.1: Artificial intelligence overview

Machine learning

Machine learning is an applied field of study within the broader subject of artificial intelligence that focuses on learning from data by detecting patterns, trends, and relationships in order to make predictions and ultimately deliver actionable insights to help decision making. Machine learning models can be split into three main types: *supervised learning, unsupervised learning,* and *reinforced learning*.

Supervised learning

In supervised learning, the goal is to learn a function that is able to map inputs x to outputs y given a labeled set of input-output pairs D, where D is referred to as the training set and N is the number of input-output pairs in the training set:

$$D = (x_1, y_1), (x_2, y_2), \ldots, (x_n, y_n) = \{(x_i, y_i)\}_{i=1}^{N}$$

In simple applications of supervised learning models, each training input x_i is a numerical vector representing model features such as price, age, and temperature. In complex applications, x_i may represent more complex objects, such as a time series, images, and text.

When the output y_i (also called the response variable) is categorical in nature, then the problem is referred to as a classification problem, where y_i belongs to a finite set consisting of K elements or possible classifications:

$$y_i \in \{1, 2, \ldots, K\}$$

When the output y_i is a real number, then the problem is referred to as a regression problem.

So what does this mean in practice? Well, the training set D is essentially a dataset for which the input features have already been mapped to an output. In other words, we already know what the answer is for the training dataset - it is *labelled*. For example, if the problem were to predict monthly sales figures for an e-commerce website based on the amount of money spent on online advertising (that is, a regression problem), the training dataset would already map advertising costs (input feature) to known monthly sales figures (output), as illustrated in *Figure 3.2*:

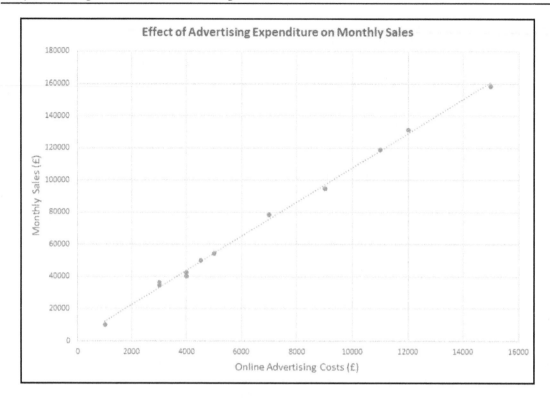

Figure 3.2: Linear regression training dataset

Supervised learning algorithms will then use this labelled training dataset to compute a mathematical function that is the best predictor of the output, given the input features. This function can then be applied to a test dataset in order to quantify its accuracy, and thereafter to a dataset that it has never seen before in order to make predictions!

Regression problems are where we want to predict a numerical outcome. Examples of regression algorithms include **Linear Regression** and **Regression Trees**, and examples of real-world use cases include price, weight, and temperature prediction. Classification problems are where we want to predict a categorical outcome. Examples of classification algorithms include **Logistic Regression**, **Multinomial Logistic Regression**, and **Classification Trees**, and examples of real-world use cases include image classification and email spam classification. We will study these algorithms in more detail in Chapter 4, *Supervised Learning Using Apache Spark*, where we will also develop supervised learning models that can be applied to real-world use cases whilst providing the ability to quantify their accuracy.

Unsupervised learning

In unsupervised learning, the goal is to uncover hidden relationships, trends, and patterns, given only the input data x_i with no output y_i. In this case, we have the following:

$$D = x_1, x_2, \ldots, x_n = \{x_i\}_{i=1}^{N}$$

In practice, this means that the emphasis is on uncovering interesting patterns and trends within a dataset in the absence of known and correct answers. Subsequently, unsupervised learning is commonly referred to as **knowledge discovery** given the fact that problems are less well-defined and we are not told what kind of patterns are contained within the data. **Clustering** is a well-known example of an unsupervised learning algorithm where the goal is to segment data points into groups, where all the data points in a specific group share similar features or attributes, as illustrated in *Figure 3.3*. Real-world use cases of clustering include document classification and clustering customers for marketing purposes:

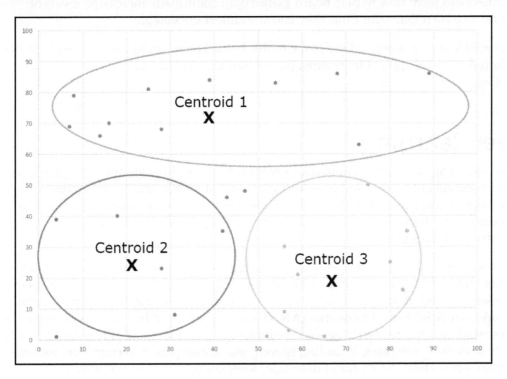

Figure 3.3: Clustering unsupervised learning model

We will study unsupervised learning algorithms in more detail in Chapter 5, *Unsupervised Learning Using Apache Spark,* including hands-on development of real-world applications.

Reinforced learning

In reinforced learning, a reward (or punishment) system is employed to impact behavior over time, based on interactions between an agent and its wider environment. An agent will receive state information from the environment and, based on that state, will perform an *action*. As a result of that action, the environment will transition to a new state that is then provided back to the agent, typically with a reward (or punishment). The goal of the agent is to therefore maximize the cumulative reward it receives. For example, consider the case of a child learning good behavior from bad behavior and being rewarded for good behavior with a treat from its parents. In the case of machines, consider the example of computer-based board game players. By combining deep learning with reinforced learning, computers can learn how to play board games with continually increasing levels of performance such that, over time, they become almost unbeatable!

Reinforced learning is beyond the scope of this book. However, to learn more about deep reinforced learning applied to gaming, please visit https://deepmind.com/blog/deep-reinforcement-learning/.

Deep learning

In deep learning, a subfield within the broader field of machine learning, the goal is still to learn a function but by employing an architecture that mimics the neural architecture found in the human brain in order to learn from experience using a hierarchy of concepts or representations. This enables us to develop more complex and powerful functions in order to predict outcomes better.

Many machine learning models employ a two-layer architecture, where some sort of function maps an input to an output. However, in the human brain, multiple layers of processing are found, in other words, a neural network. By mimicking natural neural networks, **artificial neural networks (ANN)** offer the ability to learn complex non-linear representations with no restrictions on the input features and are ideally suited to a wide variety of exciting use cases, including speech, image and pattern recognition, **natural language processing** (NLP), fraud detection, forecasting and price prediction.

Natural neuron

Deep learning algorithms mimic the neural architecture found in the human brain. If we were to study a single natural neuron in the human brain, we would find three primary areas of interest, as illustrated in *Figure 3.4*:

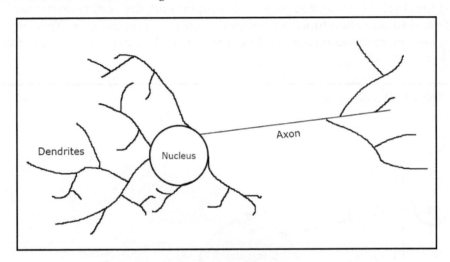

Figure 3.4: A natural neuron

Dendrites receive chemical signals and electrical impulses from other neurons that are collected and aggregated in the cell body. The nucleus, found within the cell body, is the control center of the neuron and is responsible for regulating cell functions, producing the proteins required to build new dendrites and for making the neurotransmitter chemicals used as signals. Signals can be classed as either inhibitory or excitatory. If they are inhibitory, this means that they are not transmitted to other neurons. If they are excitatory, this means that they are transmitted to other neurons via the axon. The axon is responsible for communicating signals between neurons, in some cases across distances as long as a couple of meters or a short as a few microns. The neuron therefore, as a single logical unit, is ultimately responsible for communicating information and the average human brain may contain around 100 billion neurons.

Artificial neuron

The core concepts of the natural neuron can be generalized into components of a signal processing system. In this general signal processing system, the signals received by the dendrites can be thought of as the inputs. The nucleus can be thought of as a central processing unit that collects and aggregates the inputs and, depending on the net input magnitude and an activation function, transmits outputs along the axon. This general signal processing system, modeled on a natural neuron, is called an *artificial neuron* and is illustrated in *Figure 3.5*:

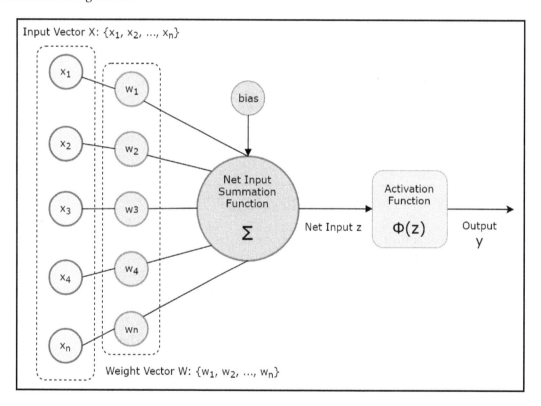

Figure 3.5: An artificial neuron

Weights

In the artificial neuron, weights can amplify or attenuate signals and are used to model the established connections to other neurons as found in the natural world. By changing the weight vectors, we can effect whether that neuron will activate or not based on the aggregation of input values with weights, called the weighted or net input z:

$$z = w_0 x_0 + w_1 x_1 + \ldots + w_n x_n = \sum_{i=0}^{n} w_i x_i = \mathbf{w}^T \mathbf{x} + bias$$

Activation function

Once the weighted input plus a bias is calculated, the **activation function**, denoted by the Greek letter *phi* (Φ), is used to determine the output of the neuron and whether it activates or not. To make this determination, an activation function is typically a non-linear function bounded between two values, thereby adding non-linearity to ANNs. As most real-world data tends to be non-linear in nature when it comes to complex use cases, we require that ANNs have the capability to learn these non-linear concepts or representations. This is enabled by non-linear activation functions. Examples of activation functions include a Heaviside step function, a sigmoid function, and a hyperbolic tangent function.

Heaviside step function

A Heaviside step function is a basic discontinuous function that compares values against a simple threshold and is used for classification where the input data is *linearly* separable. The neuron is activated if the weighted sum plus a bias exceeds a certain threshold, denoted by the Greek letter *theta* (θ) in the equation below. If it does not, the neuron is not activated. The following step function is an example of a Heaviside step function that is bounded between *1* and *-1*:

$$\phi(z) = \begin{cases} 1, & \text{if } z \geq \theta \\ -1, & \text{otherwise} \end{cases}$$

This Heaviside step function is illustrated in *Figure 3.6*:

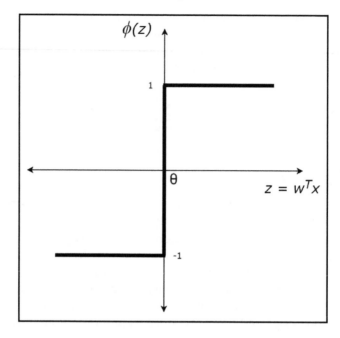

Figure 3.6: Heaviside step activation function

Sigmoid function

A sigmoid function is a non-linear mathematical function that exhibits a sigmoid curve, as illustrated in *Figure 3.7*, and often refers to the sigmoid or logistic function:

$$\phi(z) = \sigma(z) = \frac{1}{1 + e^{-z}}$$

In this case, the sigmoid activation function is bounded between 0 and 1 and is smoothly defined for *all* real input values, making it a better choice of activation function than a basic Heaviside step function. This is because, unlike the Heaviside step function, non-linear activation functions can distinguish data that is *not* linearly separable, such as image and video data. Note that by using the sigmoid function as the activation function, the artificial neuron will, in fact, correspond to a logistic regression model:

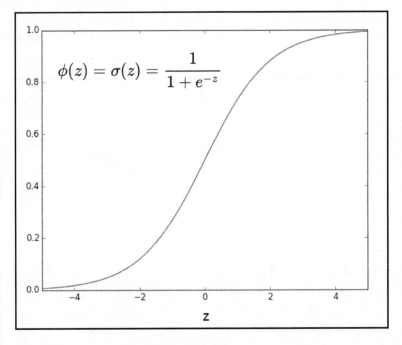

Figure 3.7: Sigmoid activation function

Hyperbolic tangent function

Finally, a hyperbolic tangent function, as illustrated in *Figure 3.8*, is the ratio between the hyperbolic sine and cosine functions:

$$\phi(z) = tanh(z) = \frac{sinh(z)}{cosh(z)} = \frac{e^z - e^{-z}}{e^z + e^{-z}}$$

In this case, an activation function based on a hyperbolic tangent function is bounded between *1* and *-1* and, similar to sigmoid functions, is smoothly defined for all real input values:

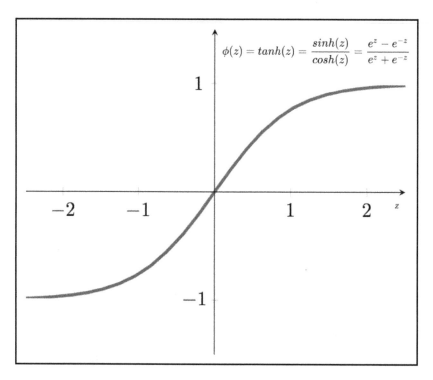

$$\phi(z) = tanh(z) = \frac{sinh(z)}{cosh(z)} = \frac{e^z - e^{-z}}{e^z + e^{-z}}$$

Figure 3.8: Hyperbolic tangent function

Artificial neural network

An **artificial neural network** (**ANN**) is a connected group of artificial neurons, where the artificial neurons are aggregated into linked **neural layers** that can be divided into three types:

- The **input layer** receives input signals from the outside world and passes these input signals to the next layer.
- **Hidden layers**, if any, perform computations on these signals and pass them to the output layer. Therefore, the outputs of the hidden layer(s) act as inputs to the final output.

- The **output layer** calculates the final output, which then influences the outside world in some manner.

Artificial neurons are linked across adjacent neural layers by **edges** that have weights associated with them. In general, the addition of more hidden neural layers increases the ability of the ANN to learn more complex concepts or representations. They are termed *hidden* because of the fact that they do not directly interact with the outside world. Note that all ANNs have an input and an output layer, with zero or more hidden layers. An ANN where signals are propagated in one direction only, in other words, signals are received by the input layer and forwarded to the next layer for processing, are called **feedforward** networks. ANNs where signals may be propagated back to artificial neurons or neural layers that have *already* processed that signal are called **feedback** networks. *Figure 3.9* illustrates the logical architecture of a feedforward ANN, where each circle represents an artificial neuron sometimes referred to as a **node** or a **unit**, and the arrows represent **edges** or **connections** between artificial neurons across adjacent neural layers:

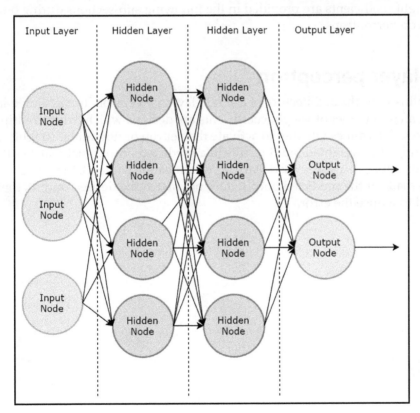

Figure 3.9: Feedforward artificial neural network

ANNs can be divided into two classes dependent on their architecture. **Mono-layer** or **single-layer** ANNs are characterized by the aggregation of all its constituent artificial neurons on the same level with no hidden layers. A single-layer perceptron is an example of a mono-layer ANN consisting of just one layer of links between input nodes and output nodes. **Multi-layer** ANNs are characterized by the segmentation of artificial neurons across multiple linked layers. A multi-layer perceptron is an example of a multi-layer ANN consisting of one or more hidden layers.

ANNs learn by optimizing their weights to deliver a desired outcome, and that by changing weights, ANNs can deliver different results for the same inputs. The goal of optimizing the weights is to minimize a **loss function**—a function that calculates the price paid for inaccurate predictions—by finding the best combination of weights that best predict the outcome. Recall that the weights represent established connections to other neurons; hence, by changing weights, ANNs are, in fact, mimicking natural neural networks by changing the connections between neurons. Various processes for learning optimal weight coefficients are provided in the following sub-sections during our discussions on perceptrons.

Single-layer perceptron

Figure 3.10 illustrates the architecture of a single-layer perceptron. In this single-layer perceptron, an optimal set of weight coefficients are derived which, when multiplied by the input features, determines whether to activate the neuron or not. Initial weights are set randomly and, if the weighted input results in a predicted output that matches the desired output (for example, in a supervised learning classification context), then no changes to the weights are made. If the predicted output does not match the desired output, then weights are updated to reduce the error.

This makes single-layer perceptrons best suited as classifiers, but only when the classes are *linearly separable*:

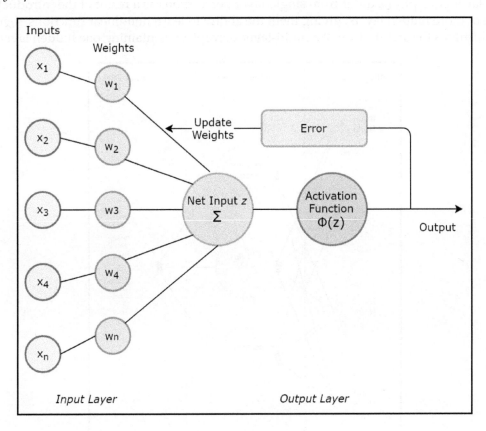

Figure 3.10: Single-layer perceptron

Multi-layer perceptron

Multi-layer perceptrons differ from single-layer perceptrons as a result of the introduction of one or more hidden layers, giving them the ability to learn non-linear functions. *Figure 3.11* illustrates the architecture of a multi-layer perceptron containing one hidden layer:

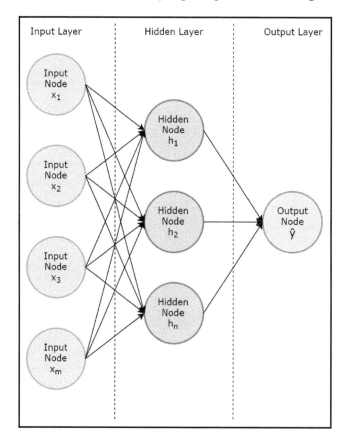

Figure 3.11: Multi-layer perceptron

Backpropagation is a supervised learning process by which multi-layer perceptrons and other ANNs can learn, that is to say, derive an optimal set of weight coefficients. The first step in backpropagation is, in fact, **forward propagation**, whereby all weights are set randomly initially and the output from the network is calculated (similar to single-layer perceptrons, but this time involving one or more hidden layers). If the predicted output does not match the desired output, the total error at the output nodes is propagated back through the entire network in an effort to readjust all weights in the network so that the error is reduced in the output layer.

Multi-layer neural networks, such as multi-layer perceptrons, are generally much more compute intensive, since the process to optimize weights involves a much greater number of weights and calculations. Therefore, training neural networks, which also typically involves a large number of data points in order to learn a large number of optimal weight coefficients, requires CPU and memory resources that previously were not readily available or cost-effective. However, with the advent of distributed systems, like those described in Chapter 1, *The Big Data Ecosystem* and the availability of cost-effective, high-performance, and resilient distributed clusters that support the processing of petabytes of data hosted by commodity hardware, research into ANNs and deep learning has exploded, as too has their application to exciting real-world artificial intelligence use cases, including the following:

- Healthcare and combating disease, including predictive diagnosis, drug discovery, and gene ontology
- Speech recognition, including language translation
- Image recognition, including visual search
- Theoretical physics and astrophysics, including satellite image classification and gravitational wave detection

In this sub-section, we have discussed two specific types of ANN, single-layer perceptrons and multi-layer perceptrons, which we will study in more detail in Chapter 7, *Deep Learning Using Apache Spark*, including the hands-on development of real-world applications. Other classes of artificial network networks include **convolutional neural networks** (also described in Chapter 7, *Deep Learning Using Apache Spark*), **recurrent neural networks**, **Kohonen self-organizing neural networks**, and **modular neural networks**, which are beyond the scope of this book. To learn more about ANNs and the exciting field of deep learning, please visit http://deeplearning.net/.

NLP

NLP refers to a family of computer science disciplines, including machine learning, linguistics, information engineering, and data management, used to analyze and understand natural languages, including speech and text. NLP can be applied to a wide variety of real-world use cases, including the following:

- **Named entity recognition** (**NER**): Automatically identifying and parsing entities from text, including people, physical addresses, and email addresses
- **Relationship extraction**: Automatically identifying the types of relationships between parsed entities

- **Machine translation and transcription**: Automatically translating from one natural language to another, for example, from English to Chinese
- **Searching**: Automatically searching across vast collections of structured, semi-structured, and unstructured documents and objects in order to fulfill a natural language query
- **Speech recognition**: Automatically deriving meaning from human speech
- **Sentiment analysis**: Automatically identifying human sentiment toward a topic or entity
- **Question answering**: Automatically answering natural, fully-formed questions

A common technique employed in NLP is developing a data engineering pipeline that pre-processes text in order to generate features for input into machine learning models. Common pre-processing techniques include **tokenization** (splitting text into smaller and simpler units called tokens, where tokens are often individual words or terms), **stemming** and **lemmatisation** (reducing tokens to a base form), and removing **stop-words** (such as *I*, *this*, and *at*). The resultant set of terms is converted into features to then feed into machine learning models. A very basic algorithm used to convert the set of terms into features is called **Bag of Words**, which simply counts the number of occurrences of each unique term, thereby converting text into numeric feature vectors.

NLP is important as it provides a means to achieve true seamless interaction between artificially intelligent systems/machines and humans, such as through conversation interfaces. We will study NLP in more detail in `Chapter 6`, *Natural Language Processing Using Apache Spark*, including the hands-on development of real-world applications.

Cognitive computing

Similar to NLP, cognitive computing actually refers to a family of computer science disciplines, including machine learning, deep learning, NLP, statistics, business intelligence, data engineering, and information retrieval that, together, are used to develop systems that simulate human thought processes. Real-world implementations of cognitive systems include chatbots and virtual assistants (such as Amazon Alexa, Google Assistant, and Microsoft Cortana) that understand natural human language and provide contextual conversation interfaces, including question-answering, personalized recommendations, and information retrieval systems.

Machine learning pipelines in Apache Spark

To end this chapter, we will take a look at how Apache Spark can be used to implement the algorithms that we have previously discussed by taking a look at how its machine learning library, MLlib, works under the hood. MLlib provides a suite of tools designed to make machine learning accessible, scalable, and easy to deploy.

 Note that as of Spark 2.0, the MLlib RDD-based API is in maintenance mode. The examples in this book will use the DataFrame-based API, which is now the primary API for MLlib. For more information, please visit https://spark.apache.org/docs/latest/ml-guide.html.

At a high level, the typical implementation of machine learning models can be thought of as an ordered pipeline of algorithms, as follows:

1. Feature extraction, transformation, and selection
2. Train a predictive model based on these feature vectors and labels
3. Make predictions using the trained predictive model
4. Evaluate model performance and accuracy

MLlib exposes two core abstractions that facilitate this high-level pipeline and allow machine learning models to be developed in Apache Spark:

- **Transformers**: Formally, a transformer converts one DataFrame (see Chapter 1, *The Big Data Ecosystem*) into another DataFrame. The new DataFrame will typically contain one or more new columns appended to it. In the context of a machine learning model, an input DataFrame may consist of a column containing the relevant feature vectors. A transformer will then take this input DataFrame and predict a label for each feature vector. The transformer will then output a new DataFrame with a new column containing the predicted labels.

- **Estimators**: Formally, an estimator abstracts a learning algorithm. In practice, an estimator is a type of learning algorithm, such as a logistic regression algorithm. In this case, the estimator is called *LogisticRegression* in MLlib. The estimator will take an input DataFrame and call the fit() method on it. The output of the fit() method, and hence the output of the estimator, will be a *trained model*. In this example, the *LogisticRegression* estimator will produce a trained *LogisticRegressionModel* model object. The model object itself is, in fact, a *transformer*, because the trained model can now take a new DataFrame containing new feature vectors and make predictions on them.

Returning to our definition of a pipeline, this can now be extended. A pipeline is, in fact, an ordered sequence of stages where each stage is either a transformer or an estimator.

Figure 3.12 illustrates a pipeline used to train a model. In *Figure 3.12*, NLP *transformations* are applied to tokenize raw training text into a set of words or terms. The tokenizer is referred to as a feature *transformer*. An algorithm called HashingTF is then applied to take the set of terms and convert it into fixed-length feature vectors (HashingTF ultimately calculates the term frequencies using a hash function). HashingTF is also a *transformer*. The *LogisticRegression* estimator is then applied to these feature vectors, via `LogisticRegression.fit()`, to generate a trained *LogisticRegressionModel*, which itself is a type of *transformer*:

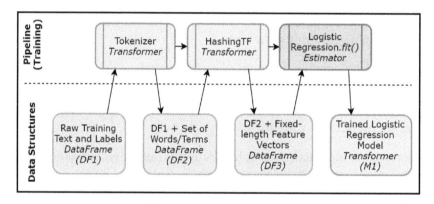

Figure 3.12: MLlib training pipeline

Figure 3.13 illustrates a pipeline used to test a model. In this diagram, similar to the training pipeline, a tokenizer feature *transformer* is used to extract terms from the raw test text, and then the HashingTF *transformer* is applied to convert the set of terms into fixed-length feature vectors. However, since we already have a trained model generated by the training pipeline in *Figure 3.12*, the feature vectors are passed as input into this trained model *transformer* in order to make predictions and output a new DataFrame containing these predictions on the test data:

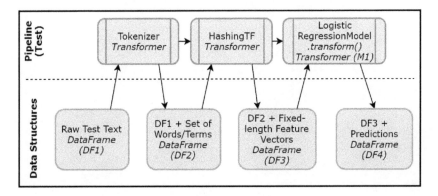

Figure 3.13: MLlib test pipeline

In addition to providing common machine learning algorithms and methods to extract, transform, and select model features and other pipeline abstractions, MLlib also exposes methods to save trained models and pipelines to an underlying filesystem that can then be loaded later on if and when required. MLlib also provides utility methods covering operations in statistics, linear algebra, and data engineering. To learn more about MLlib, please visit http://spark.apache.org/docs/latest/ml-guide.html.

Summary

In this chapter, we have defined what is meant by artificial intelligence, machine learning, and cognitive computing. We have explored common machine learning algorithms at a high level, including deep learning and ANNs, as well as taking a look at Apache Spark's machine learning library, MLlib, and how it can be used to implement these algorithms within machine learning pipelines.

In the next chapter, we will start developing, deploying, and testing supervised machine learning models applied to real-world use cases using PySpark and MLlib.

4
Supervised Learning Using Apache Spark

In this chapter, we will develop, test, and evaluate supervised machine learning models applied to a variety of real-world use cases using Python, Apache Spark, and its machine learning library, `MLlib`. Specifically, we will train, test, and interpret the following types of supervised machine learning models:

- Univariate linear regression
- Multivariate linear regression
- Logistic regression
- Classification and regression trees
- Random forests

Linear regression

The first supervised learning model that we will study is that of linear regression. Formally, linear regression models the relationship between a *dependent* variable using a set of one or more *independent* variables. The resulting model can then be used to predict the numerical value of the *dependent* variable. But what does this mean in practice? Well, let's look at our first real-world use case to make sense of this.

Case study – predicting bike sharing demand

Bike sharing schemes have become very popular across the world over the last decade or so as people seek a convenient means to travel within busy cities while limiting their carbon footprint and helping to reduce road congestion. If you are unfamiliar with bike sharing systems, they are very simple; people rent a bike from certain locations in a city and thereafter return that bike to either the same or another location once they have finished their journey. In this example, we will be examining whether we can predict the daily demand for bike sharing systems given the weather on a particular day!

 The dataset that we will be using has been derived from the **University of California's (UCI)** machine learning repository found at `https://archive.ics.uci.edu/ml/index.php`. The specific bike sharing dataset that we will use, available from both the GitHub repository accompanying this book and from `https://archive.ics.uci.edu/ml/datasets/Bike+Sharing+Dataset`, has been cited by Fanaee-T, Hadi, and Gama, Joao, 'Event labeling combining ensemble detectors and background knowledge,' Progress in Artificial Intelligence (2013): pp. 1-15, Springer Berlin Heidelberg.

If you open `bike-sharing-data/day.csv` in any text editor, from either the GitHub repository accompanying this book or from UCI's machine learning repository, you will find bike sharing data aggregated on a daily basis over 731 days using the following schema:

Column name	Data type	Description
instant	Integer	Unique record identifier (primary key)
dteday	Date	Date
season	Integer	Season (1 – spring, 2 – summer, 3 – fall, 4 – winter)
yr	Integer	Year
mnth	Integer	Month
holiday	Integer	Day is a holiday or not
weekday	Integer	Day of the week
workingday	Integer	1 – neither a weekend nor a holiday, 0 – otherwise
weathersit	Integer	1 – clear, 2 – mist, 3 – light snow, 4 – heavy rain

temp	Double	Normalized temperature in Celsius
atemp	Double	Normalized feeling temperature in Celsius
hum	Double	Normalized humidity
windspeed	Double	Normalized wind speed
casual	Integer	Count of casual users for that day
registered	Integer	Count of registered users for that day
cnt	Integer	Count of total bike renters that day

Using this dataset, can we predict the total bike renters for a given day (*cnt*) given the weather patterns for that particular day? In this case, *cnt* is the *dependent* variable that we wish to predict based on a set of *independent* variables that we shall choose from.

Univariate linear regression

Univariate (or single-variable) linear regression refers to a linear regression model where we use only one independent variable x to learn a *linear* function that maps x to our dependent variable y:

$$y^i = \beta_0 + \beta_1 x^i + \epsilon^i$$

In the preceding equation, we have the following:

- y^i represents the *dependent* variable (cnt) for the ith observation
- x^i represents the single *independent* variable for the ith observation
- ϵ^i represents the *error* term for the ith observation
- β_0 is the intercept coefficient
- β_1 is the regression coefficient for the single independent variable

Since, in general form, a univariate linear regression model is a linear function, we can easily plot this on a scatter graph where the x-axis represents the single independent variable, and the y-axis represents the dependent variable that we are trying to predict. *Figure 4.1* illustrates the scatter plot generated when we plot normalized feeling temperature (independent variable) against total daily bike renters (dependent variable):

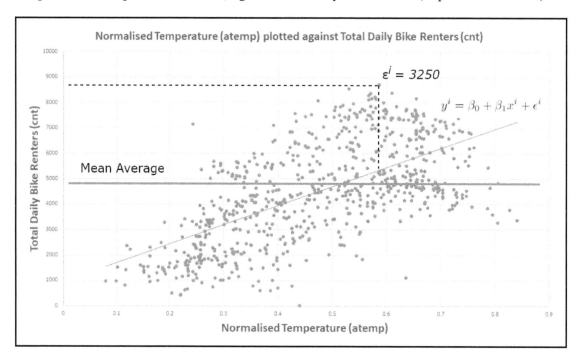

Figure 4.1: Normalized temperature against total daily bike renters

By analyzing *Figure 4.1*, you will see that there seems to be a general positive linear trend between the normalized feeling temperature (**atemp**) and the total daily biker renters (**cnt**). However, you will also see that our blue trend line, which is the visual representation of our univariate linear regression function, is not perfect, in other words, not all of our data points fit exactly on this line. In the real world, it is extremely rare to have a perfect model; in other words, all predictive models will make some mistakes. The goal therefore is to minimize the number of mistakes our models make so that we may have confidence in the predictions that they provide.

Residuals

The errors (or mistakes) that our model makes are called error terms or *residuals,* and are denoted in our univariate linear regression equation by ε^i. Our goal therefore is to choose regression coefficients for the independent variables (in our case β_1) that minimize these residuals. To compute the ith residual, we can simply subtract the predicted value from the actual value, as illustrated in *Figure 4.1*. To quantify the quality of our regression line, and hence our regression model, we can use a metric called the **Sum of Squared Errors (SSE)**, which is simply the sum of all squared residuals, as follows:

$$SSE = (\epsilon_1)^2 + (\epsilon_2)^2 + \ldots + (\epsilon_n)^2$$

A smaller SSE implies a better fit. However, SSE as a metric to quantify the quality of our regression model has its limitations. SSE scales with the number of data points N, which means that if we doubled the number of data points, the SSE may be twice as large, which may lead you to believe that the model is twice as bad, which is not the case! We therefore require other means to quantify the quality of our model.

Root mean square error

The **root mean square error** (**RMSE**) is the square root of the SSE divided by the total number of data points N, as follows:

$$RMSE = \sqrt{\frac{SSE}{N}}$$

The RMSE tends to be used more often as a means to quantify the quality of a linear regression model, since its units are the same as the dependent variable, and is normalized by N.

R-squared

Another metric that provides an error measure of a linear regression model is called the R^2 (R-squared) metric. The R^2 metric represents the proportion of *variance* in the dependent variable explained by the independent variable(s). The equation for calculating R^2 is as follows:

$$R^2 = 1 - \frac{SSE}{SST}$$

In this equation, SST refers to the **Total Sum of Squares**, which is just the SSE from the overall mean (as illustrated in *Figure 4.1* by the red horizontal line, which is often used as a **baseline** model). An R^2 value of 0 implies a linear regression model that provides no improvement over the baseline model (in other words, SSE = SST). An R^2 value of 1 implies a perfect predictive linear regression model (in other words, SSE = 0). The aim therefore is to get an R^2 value as close as possible to 1.

Univariate linear regression in Apache Spark

Returning to our case study, let's develop a univariate linear regression model in Apache Spark using its machine learning library, MLlib, in order to predict the total daily bike renters using our bike sharing dataset:

 The following sub-sections describe each of the pertinent cells in the corresponding Jupyter Notebook for this use case, entitled chp04-01-univariate-linear-regression.ipynb, and which may be found in the GitHub repository accompanying this book.

1. First, we import the required Python dependencies, including pandas (Python data analysis library), matplotlib (Python plotting library), and pyspark (Apache Spark Python API). By using the %matplotlib magic function, any plots that we generate will automatically be rendered within the Jupyter Notebook cell output:

```
%matplotlib inline
import matplotlib.pyplot as plt
import pandas as pd
import findspark
findspark.init()
from pyspark import SparkContext, SparkConf
from pyspark.sql import SQLContext
from pyspark.ml.feature import VectorAssembler
from pyspark.ml.regression import LinearRegression
from pyspark.ml.evaluation import RegressionEvaluator
```

2. Before we instantiate a Spark context, it is generally a good idea to load a sample of any pertinent dataset into pandas so that we may identify any trends or patterns before developing a predictive model. Here, we use the pandas library to load the entire CSV into a pandas DataFrame called bike_sharing_raw_df (since it is a very small dataset anyway):

```
bike_sharing_raw_df = pd.read_csv('<Path to CSV file>',
    delimiter = '<delimiter character>')
```

```
bike_sharing_raw_df.head()
```

3. In cells 3.1 to 3.4, we use the `matplotlib` library to plot various independent variables (`temp`, `atemp`, `hum`, and `windspeed`) against the dependent variable (`cnt`):

```
bike_sharing_raw_df.plot.scatter(x = '<Independent Variable>',
    y = '<Dependent Variable>')
```

As you can see in *Figure 4.2*, there is a general positive linear relationship between the normalized temperatures (`temp` and `atemp`) and the total daily bike renters (cnt). However, there is no such obvious trend when using humidity and wind speed as our independent variables. Therefore, we will proceed to develop a univariate linear regression model using normalized feeling temperature (`atemp`) as our single independent variable, with total daily bike renters (`cnt`) being our dependent variable:

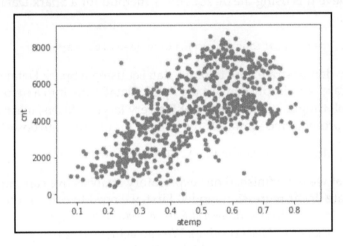

Figure 4.2: Bike sharing scatter plot

4. In order to develop a Spark application, we need to first instantiate a Spark context (as described in `Chapter 1`, *The Big Data Ecosystem*) to connect to our local Apache Spark cluster. We also instantiate a Spark `SQLContext` for the structured processing of our dataset:

```
conf = SparkConf().setMaster("spark://192.168.56.10:7077")
    .setAppName("Univariate Linear Regression - Bike Sharing")
sc = SparkContext(conf=conf)
sqlContext = SQLContext(sc)
```

5. We can now load our CSV dataset into a Spark DataFrame (see `Chapter 1`, *The Big Data Ecosystem*) called `bike_sharing_df`. We use the `SQLContext` previously defined and we tell Spark to use the first row as the header row and to infer the schema data types:

```
bike_sharing_df = sqlContext.read
    .format('com.databricks.spark.csv')
    .options(header = 'true', inferschema = 'true')
    .load('Path to CSV file')
bike_sharing_df.head(10)
bike_sharing_df.printSchema()
```

6. Before developing a predictive model, it is also a good idea to generate standard statistical metrics for a dataset so as to gain additional insights. Here, we generate the row count for the DataFrame, as well as calculating the mean average, standard deviation, and the minimum and maximum for each column. We achieve this using the `describe()` method for a Spark DataFrame as follows:

```
bike_sharing_df.describe().toPandas().transpose()
```

7. We now demonstrate how to plot a dataset using a Spark DataFrame as an input. In this case, we simply convert the Spark DataFrame into a `pandas` DataFrame before plotting as before (note that for very large datasets, it is recommended to use a representative sample of the dataset for plotting purposes):

```
bike_sharing_df.toPandas().plot.scatter(x='atemp', y='cnt')
```

8. Now that we have finished our exploratory analysis, we can start developing our univariate linear regression model! First, we need to convert our independent variable (`atemp`) into a *numerical feature vector* (see `Chapter 3`, *Artificial Intelligence and Machine Learning*). We can achieve this using MLlib's `VectorAssembler`, which will take one or more feature columns, convert them into feature vectors, and store those feature vectors in an output column, which, in this example, is called `features`:

```
univariate_feature_column = 'atemp'
univariate_label_column = 'cnt'
vector_assembler = VectorAssembler(
    inputCols = [univariate_feature_column],
    outputCol = 'features')
```

We then apply the `VectorAssembler` *transformer* (see `Chapter 3`, *Artificial Intelligence and Machine Learning*) to the raw dataset and identify the column that contains our label (in this case, our dependent variable `cnt`). The output is a new Spark DataFrame called `bike_sharing_features_df` containing our independent numerical feature vectors (`atemp`) mapped to a known label (`cnt`):

```
bike_sharing_features_df = vector_assembler
    .transform(bike_sharing_df)
    .select(['features', univariate_label_column])
bike_sharing_features_df.head(10)
```

9. As per supervised learning models in general, we need a *training* dataset to train our model in order to learn the mapping function, and a *test* dataset in order to evaluate the performance of our model. We can randomly split our raw labeled feature vector DataFrame using the `randomSplit()` method and a seed, which is used to initialize the random generator, and which can be any number you like. Note that if you use a different seed, you will get a different random split between your training and test dataset, which means that you may get slightly different coefficients for your final linear regression model:

```
train_df, test_df = bike_sharing_features_df
    .randomSplit([0.75, 0.25], seed=12345)
train_df.count(), test_df.count()
```

In our case, 75% of the original rows will form our training DataFrame called `train_df`, with the remaining 25% forming our test DataFrame called `test_df`, while using a `seed` of `12345`.

10. We are now ready to train our univariate linear regression model! We achieve this by using MLlib's `LinearRegression` estimator (see `Chapter 3`, *Artificial Intelligence and Machine Learning*) and passing it the name of the column containing our independent numerical feature vectors (in our case, called `features`) and the name of the column containing our labels (in our case, called `cnt`). We then apply the `fit()` method to train our model and output a linear regression *transformer* which, in our case, is called `linear_regression_model`:

```
linear_regression = LinearRegression(featuresCol = 'features',
    labelCol = univariate_label_column)
linear_regression_model = linear_regression.fit(train_df)
```

11. Before we evaluate our trained univariate linear regression model on the test DataFrame, let's generate some summary statistics for it. The transformer model exposes a series of statistics, including model coefficients (in other words, β_1 in our case), the intercept coefficient β_0, the error metrics RMSE and R^2, and the set of residuals for each data point. In our case, we have the following:

   - $\beta_0 = 829.62$
   - $\beta_1 = 7733.75$
   - RMSE = 1490.12
   - $R^2 = 0.42$

```
print("Model Coefficients: " +
    str(linear_regression_model.coefficients))
print("Intercept: " + str(linear_regression_model.intercept))
training_summary = linear_regression_model.summary
print("RMSE: %f" % training_summary.rootMeanSquaredError)
print("R-SQUARED: %f" % training_summary.r2)
print("TRAINING DATASET DESCRIPTIVE SUMMARY: ")
train_df.describe().show()
print("TRAINING DATASET RESIDUALS: ")
training_summary.residuals.show()
```

Therefore, our trained univariate linear regression model has learned the following function in order to be able to predict our dependent variable y (total daily bike renters) using a single independent variable x (normalized feeling temperature):

$y = 829.62 + 7733.75x$

12. Let's now apply our trained model to our test DataFrame in order to evaluate its performance on test data. Here, we apply our trained linear regression model transformer to the test DataFrame using the `transform()` method in order to make predictions. For example, our model predicts a total daily bike rental count of 1742 given a normalized feeling temperature of 0.11793. The actual total daily bike rental count was 1416 (an error of 326):

```
test_linear_regression_predictions_df =
    linear_regression_model.transform(test_df)
test_linear_regression_predictions_df
    .select("prediction", univariate_label_column, "features")
    .show(10)
```

13. We now compute the same RMSE and R^2 error metrics, but based on the performance of our model on the *test* DataFrame. In our case, these are 1534.51 (RMSE) and 0.34 (R^2) respectively, calculated using MLlib's RegressionEvaluator. So, in our case, our trained model actually performs more poorly on the test dataset:

```
linear_regression_evaluator_rmse = RegressionEvaluator(
    predictionCol = "prediction",
    labelCol = univariate_label_column, metricName = "rmse")
linear_regression_evaluator_r2 = RegressionEvaluator(
    predictionCol = "prediction",
    labelCol = univariate_label_column, metricName = "r2")
print("RMSE on Test Data = %g" % linear_regression_evaluator_rmse
    .evaluate(test_linear_regression_predictions_df))
print("R-SQUARED on Test Data = %g" %
    linear_regression_evaluator_r2
    .evaluate(test_linear_regression_predictions_df))
```

14. Note that we can generate the same metrics but using the evaluate() method of the linear regression model, as shown in the following code block:

```
test_summary = linear_regression_model.evaluate(test_df)
print("RMSE on Test Data = %g" % test_summary.rootMeanSquaredError)
print("R-SQUARED on Test Data = %g" % test_summary.r2)
```

15. Finally, we terminate our Spark application by stopping the Spark context:

```
sc.stop()
```

Multivariate linear regression

Our univariate linear regression model actually performed relatively poorly on both the training and test datasets, with R^2 values of 0.42 on the training dataset and 0.34 on the test dataset respectively. Is there any way we can take advantage of the other independent variables available in our raw dataset to increase the predictive quality of our model?

Multivariate (or multiple) linear regression extends univariate linear regression by allowing us to utilize more than one independent variable, in this case K independent variables, as follows:

$$y^i = \beta_0 + \beta_1 x_1^i + \beta_2 x_2^i + \ldots + \beta_k x_k^i + \epsilon^i$$

As before, we have our dependent variable y^i (for the ith observation), an intercept coefficient β_0, and our residuals ε^i. But we also now have k independent variables, each with their own regression coefficient, β_k. The goal, as before, is to derive coefficients that minimize the amount of error that our model makes. The problem now though is how to choose which subset of independent variables to use in order to train our multivariate linear regression model. Adding more independent variables increases the complexity of models in general and, hence, the data storage and processing requirements of underlying processing platforms. Furthermore, models that are too complex tend to cause **overfitting**, whereby the model achieves better performance (in other words, a higher R^2 metric) on the training dataset used to train the model than on new data that it has not seen before.

Correlation

Correlation is a metric that measures the linear relationship between two variables, and helps us to decide which independent variables to include in our model:

- +1 implies a perfect positive linear relationship
- 0 implies no linear relationship
- -1 implies a perfect negative linear relationship

When two variables have an *absolute* value of correlation close to 1, then these two variables are said to be "highly correlated".

Multivariate linear regression in Apache Spark

Returning to our case study, let's now develop a multivariate linear regression model in order to predict the total daily bike renters using our bike sharing dataset and a subset of independent variables:

The following sub-sections describe each of the pertinent cells in the corresponding Jupyter Notebook for this use case, entitled `chp04-02-multivariate-linear-regression.ipynb`, and which may be found in the GitHub repository accompanying this book. Note that for the sake of brevity, we will skip those cells that perform the same functions as seen previously.

1. First, let's demonstrate how we can use Spark to calculate the correlation value between our dependent variable, `cnt`, and each independent variable in our DataFrame. We achieve this by iterating over each column in our raw Spark DataFrame and using the `stat.corr()` method as follows:

```
independent_variables = ['season', 'yr', 'mnth', 'holiday',
    'weekday', 'workingday', 'weathersit', 'temp', 'atemp',
    'hum', 'windspeed']
dependent_variable = ['cnt']
bike_sharing_df = bike_sharing_df.select( independent_variables +
    dependent_variable )
for i in bike_sharing_df.columns:
    print( "Correlation to CNT for ",
        i, bike_sharing_df.stat.corr('cnt', i))
```

The resultant correlation matrix shows that the independent variables—`season`, `yr`, `mnth`, `temp`, and `atemp`, exhibit significant positive correlation with our dependent variable `cnt`. We will therefore proceed to train a multivariate linear regression model using this subset of independent variables.

2. As seen previously, we can apply a `VectorAssembler` in order to generate numerical feature vector representations of our collection of independent variables along with the `cnt` label. The syntax is identical to that seen previously, but this time we pass multiple columns to the `VectorAssembler` representing the columns containing our independent variables:

```
multivariate_feature_columns = ['season', 'yr', 'mnth',
    'temp', 'atemp']
multivariate_label_column = 'cnt'
vector_assembler = VectorAssembler(inputCols =
    multivariate_feature_columns, outputCol = 'features')
bike_sharing_features_df = vector_assembler
    .transform(bike_sharing_df)
    .select(['features', multivariate_label_column])
```

3. We are now ready to generate our respective training and test datasets using the `randomSplit` method via the DataFrame API:

```
train_df, test_df = bike_sharing_features_df
    .randomSplit([0.75, 0.25], seed=12345)
train_df.count(), test_df.count()
```

4. We can now train our multivariate linear regression model using the same `LinearRegression` estimator that we used in our univariate linear regression model:

```
linear_regression = LinearRegression(featuresCol = 'features',
    labelCol = multivariate_label_column)
linear_regression_model = linear_regression.fit(train_df)
```

5. After splitting our original DataFrame into a training and test DataFrame respectively, and applying the same *LinearRegression* estimator to the training DataFrame, we now have a trained multivariate linear regression model with the following summary training statistics (as can be seen in cell 8 of this Jupyter Notebook):

- $\beta_0 = -389.94$, $\beta_1 = 526.05$, $\beta_2 = 2058.85$, $\beta_3 = -51.90$, $\beta_4 = 2408.66$, $\beta_5 = 3502.94$
- RMSE = 1008.50
- $R^2 = 0.73$

Therefore, our trained multivariate linear regression model has learned the following function in order to be able to predict our dependent variable y (total daily bike renters) using a set of independent variables x_k (season, year, month, normalized temperature, and normalized feeling temperature):

$y = -389.94 + 526.05x_1 + 2058.85x_2 - 51.90x_3 + 2408.66x_4 + 3502.94x_5$

Furthermore, our trained multivariate linear regression model actually performs even better on the test dataset with a test RMSE of 964.60 and a test R^2 of 0.74.

To finish our discussion of multivariate linear regression models, note that our training R^2 metric will always either increase or stay the same as more independent variables are added. However, a better training R^2 metric does not always imply a better test R^2 metric—in fact, a test R^2 metric can even be negative, meaning that it performs worse on the test dataset than the baseline model (which can never be the case for the training R^2 metric). The goal therefore is to be able to develop a model that works well for both the training and test datasets.

Logistic regression

We have seen how linear regression models allows us to predict a numerical outcome. Logistic regression models, however, allow us to predict a *categorical* outcome by predicting the probability that an outcome is true.

As with linear regression, in logistic regression models, we also have a dependent variable y and a set of independent variables $x_1, x_2, ..., x_k$. In logistic regression however, we want to learn a function that provides the probability that $y = 1$ (in other words, that the outcome variable is true) given this set of independent variables, as follows:

$$P(y = 1) = \frac{1}{1 + e^{-(\beta_0 + \beta_1 x_1 + \beta_2 x_2 + ... + \beta_x x_k)}}$$

This function is called the **Logistic Response** function, and provides a number between 0 and 1, representing the probability that the outcome-dependent variable is true, as illustrated in *Figure 4.3*:

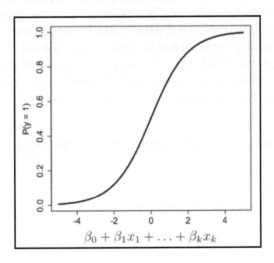

Figure 4.3: Logistic response function

Positive coefficient values β_k increase the probability that $y = 1$, and negative coefficient values decrease the probability that $y = 1$. Our goal, therefore, when developing logistic regression models, is to choose coefficients that predict a high probability when $y = 1$, but predict a low probability when $y = 0$.

Threshold value

We now know that logistic regression models provide us with the probability that the outcome variable is true, that is to say, y = 1. However, in real-world use cases, we need to make *decisions*, not just deliver probabilities. Often, we make binary predictions, such as Yes/No, Good/Bad, and Go/Stop. A threshold value (*t*) allows us to make these decisions based on probabilities as follows:

- If P(y=1) >= t, then we predict y = 1
- If P(y=1) < t, then we predict y = 0

The challenge now is how to choose a suitable value of *t*. In fact, what does *suitable* mean in this context?

In real-world use cases, some types of error are better than others. Imagine that you were a doctor and were testing a large group of patients for a particular disease using logistic regression. In this case, the outcome *y=1* would be a patient carrying the disease (therefore *y=0* would be a patient not carrying the disease), and, hence, our model would provide P(y=1) for a given person. In this example, it is better to detect as many patients potentially carrying the disease as possible, even if it means misclassifying some patients as carrying the disease who subsequently turn out not to. In this case, we select a smaller threshold value. If we select a large threshold value, however, we would detect those patients that almost certainly have the disease, but we would misclassify a large number of patients as not carrying the disease when, in actual fact, they do, which would be a much worse scenario!

In general therefore, when using logistic regression models, we can make two types of error:

- We predict y=1 (disease), but the actual outcome is y=0 (healthy)
- We predict y=0 (healthy), but the actual outcome is y=1 (disease)

Confusion matrix

A confusion (or classification) matrix can help us qualify what threshold value to use by comparing the predicted outcomes against the actual outcomes as follows:

	Predict y=0 (healthy)	Predict y=1 (disease)
Actual y=0 (healthy)	True negatives (TN)	False positives (FP)
Actual y=1 (disease)	False negatives (FN)	True positives (TP)

By generating a confusion matrix, it allows us to quantify the accuracy of our model based on a given threshold value by using the following series of metrics:

- N = number of observations
- Overall accuracy = (TN + TP) / N
- Overall error rate = (FP + FN) / N
- Sensitivity (True Positive Rate) = TP / (TP + FN)
- Specificity (True Negative Rate) = TN / (TN + FP)
- False positive error rate = FP / (TN + FP)
- False negative error rate = FN / (TP + FN)

Logistic regression models with a higher threshold value will have a lower sensitivity and higher specificity. Models with a lower threshold value will have a higher sensitivity and lower specificity. The choice of threshold value therefore depends on the type of error that is "better" for your particular use case. In use cases where there is genuinely no preference, for example, political leaning of Conservative/Non-Conservative, then you should choose a threshold value of 0.5 that will predict the most likely outcome.

Receiver operator characteristic curve

To further assist us in choosing a threshold value in a more visual way, we can generate a **receiver operator characteristic (ROC)** curve. An ROC curve plots the **false positive error rate (FPR)** against the **true positive rate (TPR**, or sensitivity) for every threshold value between 0 and 1, as illustrated in *Figure 4.4*:

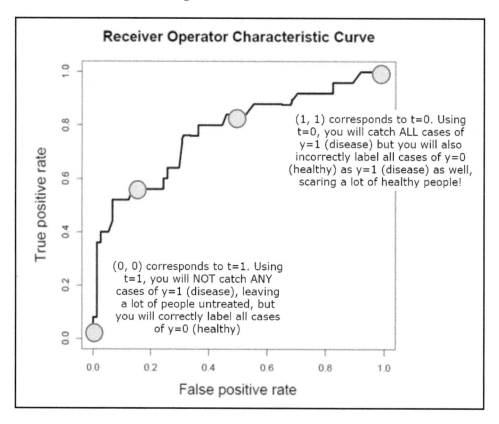

Figure 4.4: ROC curve

As illustrated in *Figure 4.4*, using a threshold value of 0 means that you will catch ALL cases of y=1 (disease), but you will also incorrectly label all cases of y=0 (healthy) as y=1 (disease) as well, scaring a lot of healthy people! However using a threshold value of 1 means that you will NOT catch ANY cases of y=1 (disease), leaving a lot of people untreated, but you will correctly label all cases of y=0 (healthy). The benefit of plotting an ROC curve therefore is that it helps you to see the trade-off for *every* threshold value, and ultimately helps you to make a decision as to which threshold value to use for your given use case.

Area under the ROC curve

As a means of quantifying the quality of the predictions made by a logistic regression model, we can calculate the **Area under the ROC curve** (**AUC**), as illustrated in *Figure 4.5*. The AUC measures the proportion of time that the model predicts correctly, with an AUC value of 1 (maximum), implying a perfect model, in other words, our model predicts correctly 100% of the time, and an AUC value of 0.5 (minimum), implying our model predicts correctly 50% of the time, analogous to just guessing:

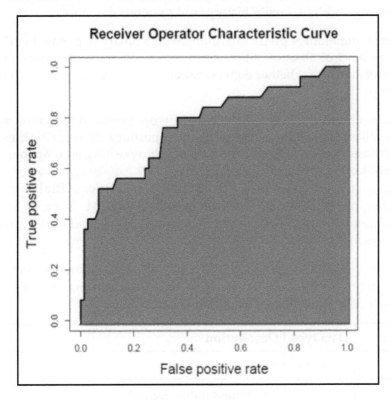

Figure 4.5: Area under the ROC curve

Case study – predicting breast cancer

Let's now apply logistic regression to a very important real-world use case; predicting patients who may have breast cancer. Approximately 1 in 8 women are diagnosed with breast cancer during their lifetime (with the disease also affecting men), resulting in the premature deaths of hundreds of thousands of women annually across the world. In fact, it is projected that over 2 million new cases of breast cancer will have been reported worldwide by the end of 2018 alone. Various factors are known to increase the risk of breast cancer, including age, weight, family history, and previous diagnoses.

Using a dataset of quantitative predictors, along with a binary dependent variable indicating the presence or absence of breast cancer, we will train a logistic regression model to predict the probability of whether a given patient is healthy (y=1) or has the biomarkers of breast cancer (y=0).

 The dataset that we will use has again been derived from the University of California's (UCI) machine learning repository. The specific breast cancer dataset, available from both the GitHub repository accompanying this book and from `https://archive.ics.uci.edu/ml/datasets/ Breast+Cancer+Coimbra`, has been cited by [Patricio, 2018] Patrício, M., Pereira, J., Crisóstomo, J., Matafome, P., Gomes, M., Seiça, R., and Caramelo, F. (2018). Using Resistin, glucose, age, and BMI to predict the presence of breast cancer. BMC Cancer, 18(1).

If you open `breast-cancer-data/dataR2.csv` in any text editor, from either the GitHub repository accompanying this book or from UCI's machine learning repository, you will find breast cancer data that employs the following schema:

Column name	Data type	Description
Age	Integer	Age of patient
BMI	Double	Body mass index (kg/m^2)
Glucose	Double	Blood glucose level (mg/dL)
Insulin	Double	Insulin level (μU/mL)
HOMA	Double	Homeostatic Model Assessment (HOMA) – used to assess β-cell function and insulin sensitivity
Leptin	Double	Hormone used to regulate energy expenditure (ng/mL)

Adiponectin	Double	Protein hormone used to regulate glucose levels (μg/mL)
Resistin	Double	Hormone that causes insulin resistance (ng/mL)
MCP.1	Double	Protein to aid recovery from injury and infection (pg/dL)
Classification	Integer	1 = Healthy patient as part of a control group, 2 = patient with breast cancer

Using this dataset, can we develop a logistic regression model that calculates the probability of a given patient being healthy (in other words, y=1) and thereafter apply a threshold value to make a predictive decision?

 The following sub-sections describe each of the pertinent cells in the corresponding Jupyter Notebook for this use case, entitled chp04-03-logistic-regression.ipynb, and which may be found in the GitHub repository accompanying this book. Note that, for the sake of brevity, we will skip those cells that perform the same functions as seen previously.

1. After loading our breast cancer CSV file, we first identify the column that will act as our label, that is to say, Classification. Since the values in this column are either 1 (healthy) or 2 (breast cancer patient), we will apply a StringIndexer to this column to identify and index all the possible categories. The result is that a label of 1 corresponds to a healthy patient, and a label of 0 corresponds to a breast cancer patient:

```
indexer = StringIndexer(inputCol = "Classification",
    outputCol = "label").fit(breast_cancer_df)
breast_cancer_df = indexer.transform(breast_cancer_df)
```

2. In our case, we will use all the raw quantitative columns [Age, BMI, Glucose, Insulin, HOMA, Leptin, Adiponectin, Resistin, and MCP.1] as independent variables in order to generate numerical feature vectors for our model. Again, we can use the VectorAssembler of MLlib to achieve this:

```
feature_columns = ['Age', 'BMI', 'Glucose', 'Insulin', 'HOMA',
    'Leptin', 'Adiponectin', 'Resistin', 'MCP_1']
label_column = 'label'
vector_assembler = VectorAssembler(inputCols = feature_columns,
    outputCol = 'features')
```

```
breast_cancer_features_df = vector_assembler
    .transform(breast_cancer_df)
    .select(['features', label_column])
```

3. After generating training and test DataFrames respectively, we apply the
`LogisticRegression` estimator of `MLlib` to train
a `LogisticRegression` model transformer:

```
logistic_regression = LogisticRegression(featuresCol = 'features',
    labelCol = label_column)
logistic_regression_model = logistic_regression.fit(train_df)
```

4. We then use our trained logistic regression model to make predictions on the test
DataFrame, using the `transform()` method of our logistic regression model
transformer. This results in a new DataFrame with the columns `rawPrediction`,
`prediction`, and `probability` appended to it. The probability of y=1, in other
words, P(y=1), is contained within the `probability` column, and the overall
predictive decision using a default threshold value of t=0.5 is contained within
the `prediction` column:

```
test_logistic_regression_predictions_df = logistic_regression_model
    .transform(test_df)
test_logistic_regression_predictions_df.select("probability",
    "rawPrediction", "prediction", label_column, "features").show()
```

5. To quantify the quality of our trained logistic regression model, we can plot an
ROC curve and calculate the AUC metric. The ROC curve is generated using
the `matplotlib` library, given the **false positive rate** (**FPR**) and **true positive
rate** (**TPR**), as exposed by evaluating our trained logistic regression model on the
test DataFrame. We can then use
`MLlib`'s `BinaryClassificationEvaluator` to calculate the AUC metric as
follows:

```
test_summary = logistic_regression_model.evaluate(test_df)
roc = test_summary.roc.toPandas()
plt.plot(roc['FPR'],roc['TPR'])
plt.ylabel('False Positive Rate')
plt.xlabel('True Positive Rate')
plt.title('ROC Curve')
plt.show()
evaluator_roc_area = BinaryClassificationEvaluator(
    rawPredictionCol = "rawPrediction", labelCol = label_column,
    metricName = "areaUnderROC")
```

```
print("Area Under ROC Curve on Test Data = %g" %
    evaluator_roc_area.evaluate(
    test_logistic_regression_predictions_df))
```

Area Under ROC Curve on Test Data = 0.859375

The resultant ROC curve, generated using the `matplotlib` library, is illustrated in *Figure 4.6*:

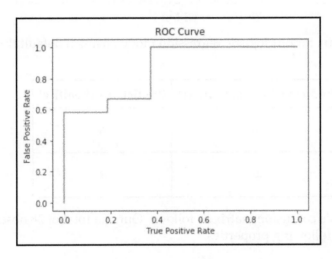

Figure 4.6: ROC curve rendered using `matplotlib`

6. One method of generating a confusion matrix based on the test dataset predictions is to simply filter the test predictions' DataFrame based on cases where the predicted outcome equals, and does not equal, the actual outcome and thereafter count the number of records post-filter:

```
N = test_logistic_regression_predictions_df.count()
true_positives = test_logistic_regression_predictions_df
    .filter( col("prediction") == 1.0 )
    .filter( col("label") == 1.0 ).count()
true_negatives = test_logistic_regression_predictions_df
    .filter( col("prediction") == 0.0 )
    .filter( col("label") == 0.0 ).count()
false_positives = test_logistic_regression_predictions_df
    .filter( col("prediction") == 1.0 )
    .filter( col("label") == 0.0 ).count()
false_negatives = test_logistic_regression_predictions_df
    .filter( col("prediction") == 0.0 )
    .filter( col("label") == 1.0 ).count()
```

7. Alternatively, we can use MLlib's RDD API (which is in maintenance mode as of Spark 2.0) to automatically generate the confusion matrix by converting the test predictions' DataFrame into an RDD (see `Chapter 1`, *The Big Data Ecosystem*), and thereafter passing it to the `MulticlassMetrics` evaluation abstraction:

```
predictions_and_label = test_logistic_regression_predictions_df
    .select("prediction", "label").rdd
metrics = MulticlassMetrics(predictions_and_label)
print(metrics.confusionMatrix())
```

The confusion matrix for our logistic regression model, using a default threshold value of 0.5, is as follows:

	Predict y=0 (breast cancer)	**Predict y=1 (healthy)**
Actual y=0 (breast cancer)	10	6
Actual y=1 (healthy)	4	8

We can interpret this confusion matrix as follows. Out of a total of 28 observations, our model exhibits the following properties:

- Correctly labeling 10 cases of breast cancer that actually are breast cancer
- Correctly labeling 8 healthy patients that actually are healthy patients
- Incorrectly labeling 6 patients as healthy when they actually have breast cancer
- Incorrectly labeling 4 patients as having breast cancer when they are actually healthy patients
- Overall accuracy = 64%
- Overall error rate = 36%
- Sensitivity = 67%
- Specificity = 63%

To improve our logistic regression model, we must, of course, include many more observations. Furthermore, the AUC metric for our model is 0.86, which is quite high. However, bear in mind that the AUC is a measure of accuracy, taking into account all possible threshold values, while the preceding confusion matrix only takes into account a single threshold value (in this case 0.5). As an extension exercise, generate confusion matrices for a range of threshold values to see how this affects our final classifications!

Classification and Regression Trees

We have seen how linear regression models allow us to predict a numerical outcome, and how logistic regression models allow us to predict a categorical outcome. However, both of these models assume a *linear* relationship between variables. **Classification and Regression Trees (CART)** overcome this problem by generating **Decision Trees**, which are also much easier to interpret compared to the supervised learning models we have seen so far. These decision trees can then be traversed to come to a final decision, where the outcome can either be numerical (regression trees) or categorical (classification trees). A simple classification tree used by a mortgage lender is illustrated in *Figure 4.7*:

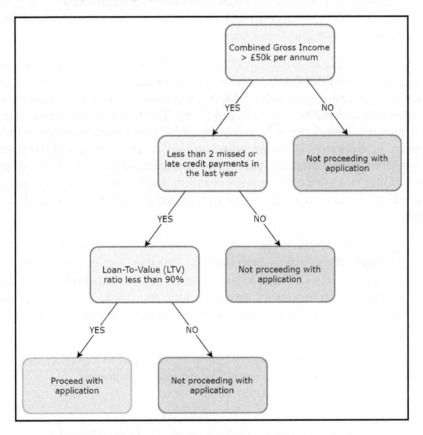

Figure 4.7: Simple classification tree used by a mortgage lender

When traversing decision trees, start at the top. Thereafter, traverse left for yes, or positive responses, and traverse right for no, or negative responses. Once you reach the end of a branch, the leaf nodes describe the final outcome.

Case study – predicting political affiliation

For our next use case, we will use congressional voting records from the US House of Representatives to build a classification tree in order to predict whether a given congressman or woman is a Republican or a Democrat.

The specific congressional voting dataset that we will use is available from both the GitHub repository accompanying this book and UCI's machine learning repository at `https://archive.ics.uci.edu/ml/datasets/congressional+voting+records`. It has been cited by Dua, D., and Karra Taniskidou, E. (2017). UCI Machine Learning Repository [http://archive.ics.uci.edu/ml]. Irvine, CA: University of California, School of Information and Computer Science.

If you open `congressional-voting-data/house-votes-84.data` in any text editor of your choosing, from either the GitHub repository accompanying this book or from UCI's machine learning repository, you will find 435 congressional voting records, of which 267 belong to Democrats and 168 belong to Republicans. The first column contains the label string, in other words, Democrat or Republican, and the subsequent columns indicate how the congressman or woman in question voted on particular key issues at the time (y = for, n = against, ? = neither for nor against), such as an anti-satellite weapons test ban and a reduction in funding to a synthetic fuels corporation. Let's now develop a classification tree in order to predict the political affiliation of a given congressman or woman based on their voting records:

The following sub-sections describe each of the pertinent cells in the corresponding Jupyter Notebook for this use case, entitled `chp04-04-classification-regression-trees.ipynb`, and which may be found in the GitHub repository accompanying this book. Note that for the sake of brevity, we will skip those cells that perform the same functions as seen previously.

1. Since our raw data file has no header row, we need to explicitly define its schema before we can load it into a Spark DataFrame, as follows:

```
schema = StructType([
    StructField("party", StringType()),
    StructField("handicapped_infants", StringType()),
    StructField("water_project_cost_sharing", StringType()),
    ...
])
```

2. Since all of our columns, both the label and all the independent variables, are string-based data types, we need to apply a *StringIndexer* to them (as we did when developing our logistic regression model) in order to identify and index all possible categories for each column before generating numerical feature vectors. However, since we have multiple columns that we need to index, it is more efficient to build a *pipeline*. A pipeline is a list of data and/or machine learning transformation stages to be applied to a Spark DataFrame. In our case, each stage in our pipeline will be the indexing of a different column as follows:

```
categorical_columns = ['handicapped_infants',
    'water_project_cost_sharing', ...]
pipeline_stages = []
for categorial_column in categorical_columns:
    string_indexer = StringIndexer(inputCol = categorial_column,
        outputCol = categorial_column + 'Index')
    encoder = OneHotEncoderEstimator(
        inputCols = [string_indexer.getOutputCol()],
        outputCols = [categorial_column + "classVec"])
    pipeline_stages += [string_indexer, encoder]

label_string_idx = StringIndexer(inputCol = 'party',
    outputCol = 'label')
pipeline_stages += [label_string_idx]
vector_assembler_inputs = [c + "classVec" for c
    in categorical_columns]
vector_assembler = VectorAssembler(
    inputCols = vector_assembler_inputs,
    outputCol = "features")
pipeline_stages += [vector_assembler]
```

3. Next, we instantiate our pipeline by passing to it the list of stages that we generated in the previous cell. We then execute our pipeline on the raw Spark DataFrame using the `fit()` method, before proceeding to generate our numerical feature vectors using `VectorAssembler` as before:

```
pipeline = Pipeline(stages = pipeline_stages)
pipeline_model = pipeline.fit(congressional_voting_df)
label_column = 'label'
congressional_voting_features_df = pipeline_model
    .transform(congressional_voting_df)
    .select(['features', label_column, 'party'])
pd.DataFrame(congressional_voting_features_df.take(5),
columns=congressional_voting_features_df.columns).transpose()
```

4. We are now ready to train our classification tree! To achieve this, we can use MLlib's `DecisionTreeClassifier` estimator to train a decision tree on our training dataset as follows:

```
decision_tree = DecisionTreeClassifier(featuresCol = 'features',
    labelCol = label_column)
decision_tree_model = decision_tree.fit(train_df)
```

5. After training our classification tree, we will evaluate its performance on the test DataFrame. As with logistic regression, we can use the AUC metric as a measure of the proportion of time that the model predicts correctly. In our case, our model has an AUC metric of 0.91, which is very high:

```
evaluator_roc_area = BinaryClassificationEvaluator(
    rawPredictionCol = "rawPrediction", labelCol = label_column,
    metricName = "areaUnderROC")
print("Area Under ROC Curve on Test Data = %g" %
evaluator_roc_area.evaluate(test_decision_tree_predictions_df))
```

6. Ideally, we would like to visualize our classification tree. Unfortunately, there is not yet any direct method in which to render a Spark decision tree without using third-party tools such as https://github.com/julioasotodv/spark-tree-plotting. However, we can render a text-based decision tree by invoking the `toDebugString` method on our trained classification tree model, as follows:

```
print(str(decision_tree_model.toDebugString))
```

With an AUC value of 0.91, we can say that our classification tree model performs very well on the test data and is very good at predicting the political affiliation of congressmen and women based on their voting records. In fact, it classifies correctly 91% of the time across all threshold values!

Note that a CART model also generates probabilities, just like a logistic regression model. Therefore, we use a threshold value (default 0.5) in order to convert these probabilities into decisions, or classifications as in our example. There is, however, an added layer of complexity when it comes to training CART models—how do we control the number of splits in our decision tree? One method is to set a lower limit for the number of training data points to put into each subset or bucket. In `MLlib`, this value is tuneable, via the `minInstancesPerNode` parameter, which is accessible when training our `DecisionTreeClassifier`. The smaller this value, the more splits that will be generated.

However, if it is too small, then overfitting will occur. Conversely, if it is too large, then our CART model will be too simple with a low level of accuracy. We will discuss how to select an appropriate value during our introduction to random forests next. Note that MLlib also exposes other configurable parameters, including maxDepth (the maximum depth of the tree) and maxBins, but note that the larger a tree becomes in terms of splits and depth, the more computationally expensive it is to compute and traverse. To learn more about the tuneable parameters available to a DecisionTreeClassifier, please visit https://spark.apache.org/docs/latest/ml-classification-regression.html.

Random forests

One method of improving the accuracy of CART models is to build multiple decision trees, not just the one. In random forests, we do just that—a large number of CART trees are generated and thereafter, each tree in the forest votes on the outcome, with the majority outcome taken as the final prediction.

To generate a random forest, a process known as bootstrapping is employed whereby the training data for each tree making up the forest is selected randomly with replacement. Therefore, each individual tree will be trained using a different subset of independent variables and, hence, different training data.

K-Fold cross validation

Let's now return to the challenge of choosing an appropriate lower-bound bucket size for an individual decision tree. This challenge is particularly pertinent when training a random forest since the computational complexity increases with the number of trees in the forest. To choose an appropriate minimum bucket size, we can employ a process known as K-Fold cross validation, the steps of which are as follows:

- Split a given training dataset into K subsets or "folds" of equal size.
- (K - 1) folds are then used to train the model, with the remaining fold, called the validation set, used to test the model and make predictions for each lower-bound bucket size value under consideration.
- This process is then repeated for all possible training and test fold combinations, resulting in the generation of multiple trained models that have been tested on each fold for every lower-bound bucket size value under consideration.

- For each lower-bound bucket size value under consideration, and for each fold, calculate the accuracy of the model on that combination pair.
- Finally, for each fold, plot the calculated accuracy of the model against each lower-bound bucket size value, as illustrated in *Figure 4.8*:

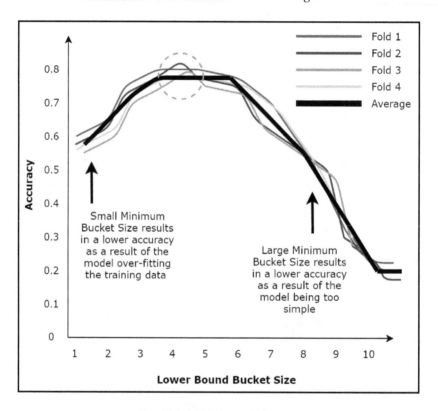

Figure 4.8: Typical K-Fold cross-validation output

As illustrated in *Figure 4.8*, choosing a small lower-bound bucket size value results in lower accuracy as a result of the model overfitting the training data. Conversely, choosing a large lower-bound bucket size value also results in lower accuracy as the model is too simple. Therefore, in our case, we would choose a lower-bound bucket size value of around 4 or 5, since the average accuracy of the model seems to be maximized in that region (as illustrated by the dashed circle in *Figure 4.8*).

Returning to our Jupyter Notebook, chp04-04-classification-regression-trees.ipynb, let's now train a random forest model using the same congressional voting dataset to see whether it results in a better performing model compared to our single classification tree that we developed previously:

1. To build a random forest, we can use MLlib's RandomForestClassifier estimator to train a random forest on our training dataset, specifying the minimum number of instances each child must have after a split via the minInstancesPerNode parameter, as follows:

```
random_forest = RandomForestClassifier(featuresCol = 'features',
    labelCol = label_column, minInstancesPerNode = 5)
random_forest_model = random_forest.fit(train_df)
```

2. We can now evaluate the performance of our trained random forest model on our test dataset by computing the AUC metric using the same BinaryClassificationEvaluator as follows:

```
test_random_forest_predictions_df = random_forest_model
    .transform(test_df)
evaluator_rf_roc_area = BinaryClassificationEvaluator(
    rawPredictionCol = "rawPrediction", labelCol = label_column,
    metricName = "areaUnderROC")
print("Area Under ROC Curve on Test Data = %g" %
evaluator_rf_roc_area.evaluate(test_random_forest_predictions_df))
```

Our trained random forest model has an AUC value of 0.97, meaning that it is more accurate in predicting political affiliation based on historical voting records than our single classification tree!

Summary

In this chapter, we have developed, tested, and evaluated various supervised machine learning models in Apache Spark using a wide variety of real-world use cases, from predicting breast cancer to predicting political affiliation based on historical voting records.

In the next chapter, we will develop, test, and evaluate unsupervised machine learning models!

5

Unsupervised Learning Using Apache Spark

In this chapter, we will train and evaluate unsupervised machine learning models applied to a variety of real-world use cases, again using Python, Apache Spark, and its machine learning library, `MLlib`. Specifically, we will develop and interpret the following types of unsupervised machine learning models and techniques:

- Hierarchical clustering
- K-means clustering
- Principal component analysis

Clustering

As described in `Chapter 3`, *Artificial Intelligence and Machine Learning*, in unsupervised learning, the goal is to uncover hidden relationships, trends, and patterns given only the input data, x_i, with no output, y_i. In other words, our input dataset will be of the following form:

$$D = x_1, x_2, \ldots, x_n = \{x_i\}_{i=1}^{n}$$

Clustering is a well-known example of a class of unsupervised learning algorithms where the goal is to segment data points into groups, where all of the data points in a specific group share similar features or attributes in common. By the nature of clustering, however, it is recommended that clustering models are trained on large datasets to avoid over fitting. The two most commonly used clustering algorithms are **hierarchical clustering** and **k-means clustering**, which are differentiated from each other by the processes by which they construct clusters. We shall study both of these algorithms in this chapter.

Euclidean distance

By definition, in order to cluster data points into groups, we require an understanding of the *distance* between two given data points. A common measure of distance is the **Euclidean distance**, which is simply the straight-line distance between two given points in *k*-dimensional space, where *k* is the number of independent variables or features. Formally, the Euclidean distance between two points, *p* and *q*, given *k* independent variables or dimensions is defined as follows:

$$d(p,q) = \sqrt{(q_1 - p_1)^2 + (q_2 - p_2)^2 + \ldots + (p_k - q_k)^2} = \sqrt{\sum_{i=1}^{k}(q_i - p_i)^2}$$

Other common measures of distance include the **Manhattan distance**, which is the sum of the absolute values instead of squares ($|q_1 - p_1| + |q_2 - p_2| + \ldots + |q_k - p_k|$) and the **maximum coordinate distance**, where measurements are only considered for those data points that deviate the most. For the remainder of this chapter, we will measure the Euclidean distance. Now that we have an understanding of distance, we can define the following measures between two clusters, as illustrated in *Figure 5.1*:

- The *minimum distance* between clusters is the distance between the two points that are the closest to each other.
- The *maximum distance* between clusters is the distance between the two points that are furthest away from each other.
- The *centroid distance* between clusters is the distance between the centroids of each cluster, where the centroid is defined as the average of all data points in a given cluster:

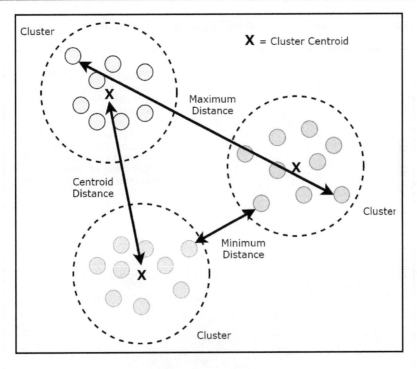

Figure 5.1: Cluster distance measures

Hierarchical clustering

In hierarchical clustering, each data point starts off in its own self-defined cluster—for example, if you have 10 data points in your dataset, then there will initially be 10 clusters. The two *nearest* clusters, as defined by the Euclidean centroid distance, for example, are then combined. This process is then repeated for all distinct clusters until eventually all data points belong in the same cluster.

This process can be visualized using a **dendrogram**, as illustrated in *Figure 5.2*:

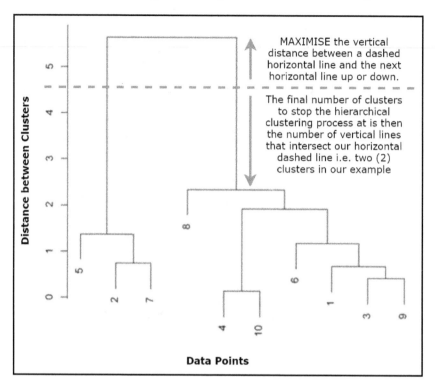

Figure 5.2: Hierarchical clustering dendrogram

A dendrogram helps us to decide when to stop the hierarchical clustering process. It is generated by plotting the original data points on the *x* axis and the distance between clusters on the *y* axis. As new parent clusters are created, by combining the nearest clusters together, a horizontal line is plotted between those child clusters. Eventually, the dendrogram ends when all data points belong in the same cluster. The aim of the dendrogram is to tell us when to stop the hierarchical clustering process. We can deduce this by drawing a dashed horizontal line across the dendrogram, placed at a position that maximizes the vertical distance between this dashed horizontal line and the next horizontal line (up or down). The final number of clusters at which to stop the hierarchical clustering process is then the number of vertical lines the dashed horizontal line intersects. In *Figure 5.2*, we would end up with two clusters containing the data points {5, 2, 7} and {8, 4, 10, 6, 1, 3, 9} respectively. However, make sure that the final number of clusters makes sense in the context of your use case.

K-means clustering

In k-means clustering, a different process is followed in order to segment data points into clusters. First, the final number of clusters, k, must be defined upfront based on the context of your use case. Once defined, each data point is randomly assigned to one of these k clusters, after which the following process is employed:

- The centroid of each cluster is computed
- Data points are then reassigned to those clusters that have the closest centroid to them
- The centroids of all clusters are then recomputed
- Data points are then reassigned once more

This process is repeated until no data points can be reassigned—that is, until there are no further improvements to be had and all data points belong to a cluster that has the closest centroid to them. Therefore, since the centroid of a cluster is defined as the mean average of all data points in a given cluster, k-means clustering effectively partitions the data points into k clusters with each data point assigned to a cluster with a mean average that is closest to it.

Note that in both clustering processes (hierarchical and k-means), a measure of distance needs to be computed. However, distance scales differently based on the type and units of the independent variables involved—for example, height and weight. Therefore, it is important to normalize your data first (sometimes called feature scaling) before training a clustering model so that it works properly. To learn more about normalization, please visit `https://en.wikipedia.org/wiki/Feature_scaling`.

Case study – detecting brain tumors

Let's apply k-means clustering to a very important real-world use case: detecting brain tumors from **magnetic resonance imaging** (**MRI**) scans. MRI scans are used across the world to generate detailed images of the human body, and can be used for a wide range of medical applications, from detecting cancerous cells to measuring blood flow. In this case study, we will use grayscale MRI scans of a healthy human brain as the input for a k-means clustering model. We will then apply the trained k-means clustering model to an MRI scan of another human brain to see if we can detect suspicious growths and tumors.

Note that the images we will use in this case study are relatively simple, in that any suspicious growths that are present will be visible to the naked eye. The fundamental purpose of this case study is to show how Python may be used to manipulate images, and how `MLlib` may be used to natively train k-means clustering models via its k-means estimator.

Feature vectors from images

The first challenge for us is to convert images into numerical feature vectors in order to train our k-means clustering model. In our case, we will be using grayscale MRI scans. A grayscale image in general can be thought of as a matrix of pixel-intensity values between 0 (black) and 1 (white), as illustrated in *Figure 5.3*:

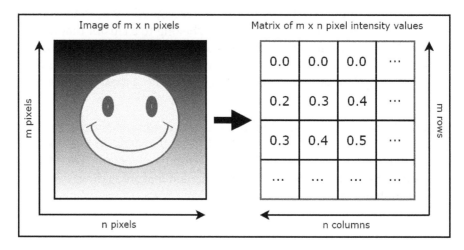

Figure 5.3: Grayscale image mapped to a matrix of pixel-intensity values

The dimensions of the resulting matrix is equal to the height (m) and width (n) of the original image in pixels. The input into our k-means clustering model will therefore be (m x n) observations across one independent variable—the pixel-intensity value. This can subsequently be represented as a single vector containing (m x n) numerical elements—that is, (**0.0, 0.0, 0.0, 0.2, 0.3, 0.4, 0.3, 0.4, 0.5** ...).

Image segmentation

Now that we have derived feature vectors from our grayscale MRI image, our k-means clustering model will assign each pixel-intensity value to one of the k clusters when we train it on our MRI scan of a healthy human brain. In the context of the real world, these k clusters represent different substances in the brain, such as grey matter, white matter, fatty tissue, and cerebral fluids, which our model will partition based on color, a process called image segmentation. Once we have trained our k-means clustering model on a healthy human brain and identified k distinct clusters, we can then apply those defined clusters to MRI brain scans of other patients in an attempt to identify the presence and volume of suspicious growths.

K-means cost function

One of the challenges when using the k-means clustering algorithm is how to choose a suitable value for k upfront, especially if it is not obvious from the wider context of the use case in question. One method to help us is to plot a range of possible values of k on the x axis against the output of the k-means cost function on the y axis. The k-means cost function computes the total sum of the squared distance of every point to its corresponding cluster centroid for that value of k. The goal is to choose a suitable value of k that minimizes the cost function, but that is not so large that it increases the computational complexity of generating the clusters with only a small return in the reduction in cost. We will demonstrate how to generate this plot, and hence choose a suitable value of k, when we develop our Spark application for image segmentation in the next subsection.

K-means clustering in Apache Spark

The MRI brain scans that we will use for our k-means clustering model have been downloaded from **The Cancer Imaging Archive (TCIA)**, a service that anonymizes and hosts a large archive of medical images of cancer for public download, and that may be found at http://www.cancerimagingarchive.net/.

The MRI scan of our healthy human brain may be found in the GitHub repository accompanying this book, and is called `mri-images-data/mri-healthy-brain.png`. The MRI scan of the test human brain is called `mri-images-data/mri-test-brain.png`. We will use both in the following Spark application when training our k-means clustering model and applying it to image segmentation. Let's begin:

> The following subsections describe each of the pertinent cells in the corresponding Jupyter notebook for this use case, called `chp05-01-kmeans-clustering.ipynb`. It can be found in the GitHub repository accompanying this book.

1. Let's open the grayscale MRI scan of the healthy human brain and take a look at it! We can achieve this using the `scikit-learn` machine learning library for Python as follows:

```
mri_healthy_brain_image = io.imread(
    'chapter05/data/mri-images-data/mri-healthy-brain.png')
mri_healthy_brain_image_plot = plt.imshow(
    mri_healthy_brain_image, cmap='gray')
```

The rendered image is illustrated in *Figure 5.4*:

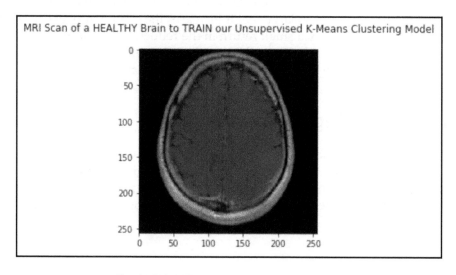

Figure 5.4: Original MRI scan rendered using scikit-learn and matplotlib

2. We now need to turn this image into a matrix of decimal point pixel-intensity values between 0 and 1. Conveniently, this function is provided out of the box by `scikit-learn` using the `img_as_float` method, as shown in the following code. The dimensions of the resulting matrix are 256 x 256, implying an original image of 256 x 256 pixels:

```
mri_healthy_brain_matrix = img_as_float(mri_healthy_brain_image)
```

3. Next, we need to flatten this matrix into a single vector of 256 x 256 elements, where each element represents a pixel-intensity value. This can be thought of as another matrix of dimensions 1 x (256 x 256) = 1 x 65536. We can achieve this using the `numpy` Python library. First, we convert our original 256 x 256 matrix into a 2-dimensional `numpy` array. We then use `numpy`'s `ravel()` method to flatten this 2-dimensional array into a 1-dimensional array. Finally, we represent this 1-dimensional array as a specialized array, or matrix, of dimensions 1 x 65536 using the `np.matrix` command, as follows:

```
mri_healthy_brain_2d_array = np.array(mri_healthy_brain_matrix)
    .astype(float)
mri_healthy_brain_1d_array = mri_healthy_brain_2d_array.ravel()
mri_healthy_brain_vector = np.matrix(mri_healthy_brain_1d_array)
```

4. Now that we have our single vector, represented as a matrix of 1 x 65536 in dimension, we need to convert it into a Spark dataframe. To achieve this, we firstly transpose the matrix using numpy's `reshape()` method so that it is 65536 x 1. We then use the `createDataFrame()` method, exposed by Spark's SQLContext, to create a Spark dataframe containing 65536 observations/rows and 1 column, representing 65536 pixel-intensity values, as shown in the following code:

```
mri_healthy_brain_vector_transposed = mri_healthy_brain_vector
    .reshape(mri_healthy_brain_vector.shape[1],
    mri_healthy_brain_vector.shape[0])
mri_healthy_brain_df = sqlContext.createDataFrame(
    pd.DataFrame(mri_healthy_brain_vector_transposed,
    columns = ['pixel_intensity']))
```

5. We are now ready to generate `MLlib` feature vectors using `VectorAssembler`, a method that we have seen before. The `feature_columns` for `VectorAssembler` will simply be the sole pixel-intensity column from our Spark dataframe. The output of applying `VectorAssembler` to our Spark dataframe via the `transform()` method will be a new Spark dataframe called `mri_healthy_brain_features_df`, containing our 65536 `MLlib` feature vectors, as follows:

```
feature_columns = ['pixel_intensity']
vector_assembler = VectorAssembler(inputCols = feature_columns,
    outputCol = 'features')
mri_healthy_brain_features_df = vector_assembler
    .transform(mri_healthy_brain_df).select('features')
```

6. We can now compute and plot the output of the k-means cost function for a range of *k* in order to determine the best value of *k* for this use case. We achieve this by using `MLlib`'s `KMeans()` estimator in the Spark dataframe containing our feature vectors, iterating over values of k in the `range(2, 20)`. We can then plot this using the `matplotlib` Python library, as shown in the following code:

```
cost = np.zeros(20)
for k in range(2, 20):
    kmeans = KMeans().setK(k).setSeed(1).setFeaturesCol("features")
    model = kmeans.fit(mri_healthy_brain_features_df
        .sample(False, 0.1, seed=12345))
    cost[k] = model.computeCost(mri_healthy_brain_features_df)

fig, ax = plt.subplots(1, 1, figsize =(8, 6))
ax.plot(range(2, 20),cost[2:20])
ax.set_title('Optimal Number of Clusters K based on the
    K-Means Cost Function for a range of K')
ax.set_xlabel('Number of Clusters K')
ax.set_ylabel('K-Means Cost')
```

Based on the resulting plot, as illustrated in *Figure 5.5*, a value of *k* of either 5 or 6 would seem to be ideal. At these values, the k-means cost is minimized with little return gained thereafter, as shown in the following graph:

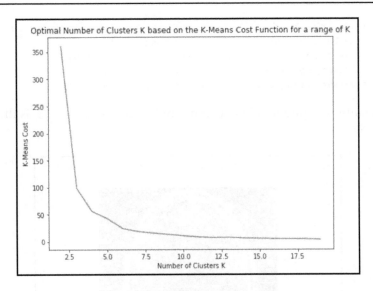

Figure 5.5: K-means cost function

7. We are now ready to train our k-means clustering model! Again, we will use `MLlib`'s `KMeans()` estimator, but this time using a defined value for *k* (5, in our case, as we decided in step 6). We will then apply it, via the `fit()` method, to the Spark dataframe containing our feature vectors and study the centroid values for each of our 5 resulting clusters, as follows:

```
k = 5
kmeans = KMeans().setK(k).setSeed(12345).setFeaturesCol("features")
kmeans_model = kmeans.fit(mri_healthy_brain_features_df)
kmeans_centers = kmeans_model.clusterCenters()
print("Healthy MRI Scan - K-Means Cluster Centers: \n")
for center in kmeans_centers:
    print(center)
```

8. Next, we will apply our trained k-means model to the Spark dataframe containing our feature vectors so that we may assign each of the 65536 pixel-intensity values to one of the five clusters. The result will be a new Spark dataframe containing our feature vectors mapped to a prediction, where in this case the prediction is simply a value between 0 and 4, representing one of the five clusters. Then, we convert this new dataframe into a 256 x 256 matrix so that we can visualize the segmented image, as follows:

```
mri_healthy_brain_clusters_df = kmeans_model
    .transform(mri_healthy_brain_features_df)
    .select('features', 'prediction')
```

```
mri_healthy_brain_clusters_matrix = mri_healthy_brain_clusters_df
    .select("prediction").toPandas().values
    .reshape(mri_healthy_brain_matrix.shape[0],
        mri_healthy_brain_matrix.shape[1])
plt.imshow(mri_healthy_brain_clusters_matrix)
```

The resulting segmented image, rendered using `matplotlib`, is illustrated in *Figure 5.6*:

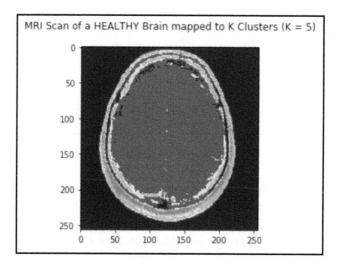

Figure 5.6: Segmented MRI scan

9. Now that we have our five defined clusters, we can apply our trained k-means model to a *new* image in order to segment it, also based on the same five clusters. First, we load the new grayscale MRI brain scan belonging to the test patient using the `scikit-learn` library, as we did before using the following code:

```
mri_test_brain_image = io.imread(
    'chapter05/data/mri-images-data/mri-test-brain.png')
```

10. Once we have loaded the new MRI brain scan image, we need to follow the same process to convert it into a Spark dataframe containing feature vectors representing the pixel-intensity values of the new test image. We then apply the trained k-means model, via the `transform()` method, to this test Spark dataframe in order to assign its pixels to one of the five clusters. Finally, we convert the Spark dataframe containing the test image predictions in to a matrix so that we can visualize the segmented test image, as follows:

```
mri_test_brain_df = sqlContext
    .createDataFrame(pd.DataFrame(mri_test_brain_vector_transposed,
    columns = ['pixel_intensity']))
mri_test_brain_features_df = vector_assembler
    .transform(mri_test_brain_df)
    .select('features')
mri_test_brain_clusters_df = kmeans_model
    .transform(mri_test_brain_features_df)
    .select('features', 'prediction')
mri_test_brain_clusters_matrix = mri_test_brain_clusters_df
    .select("prediction").toPandas().values.reshape(
    mri_test_brain_matrix.shape[0], mri_test_brain_matrix.shape[1])
plt.imshow(mri_test_brain_clusters_matrix)
```

The resulting segmented image belonging to the test patient, again rendered using `matplotlib`, is illustrated in *Figure 5.7*:

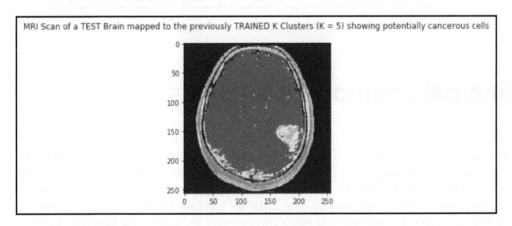

Figure 5.7: Segmented MRI scan belonging to the test patient

If we compare the two segmented images side by side (as illustrated in *Figure 5.8*), we will see that, as a result of our k-means clustering model, five different colors have been rendered representing the five different clusters. In turn, these five different clusters represent different substances in the human brain, partitioned by color. We will also see that, in the test MRI brain scan, one of the colors takes up a substantially larger area compared to the healthy MRI brain scan, pointing to a suspicious growth that may potentially be a tumor requiring further analysis, as shown in the following image:

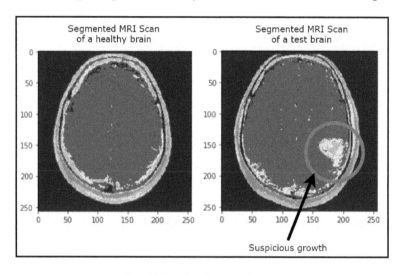

Figure 5.8: Comparison of segmented MRI scans

Principal component analysis

There are numerous real-world use cases where the number of features available that may potentially be used to train a model is very large. A common example is economic data, and using its constituent stock price data, employment data, banking data, industrial data, and housing data together to predict the **gross domestic product** (**GDP**). Such types of data are said to have high dimensionality. Though they offer numerous features that can be used to model a given use case, high-dimensional datasets increase the computational complexity of machine learning algorithms, and more importantly may also result in over fitting. Over fitting is one of the results of the **curse of dimensionality**, which formally describes the problem of analyzing data in high-dimensional spaces (which means that the data may contain many attributes, typically hundreds or even thousands of dimensions/features), but where that analysis no longer holds true in a lower-dimensional space.

Informally, it describes the value of additional dimensions at the cost of model performance. **Principal component analysis** (**PCA**) is an *unsupervised* technique used to preprocess and reduce the dimensionality of high-dimensional datasets while preserving the original structure and relationships inherent to the original dataset so that machine learning models can still learn from them and be used to make accurate predictions.

Case study – movie recommendation system

To better understand PCA, let's study a movie recommendation use case. Our aim is to build a system that can make personalized movie recommendations to users based on historic user-community movie ratings (note that user viewing history data could also be used for such a system, but this is beyond the scope of this example).

The historic user-community movie ratings data that we will use for our case study has been downloaded from GroupLens, a research laboratory based at the University of Minnesota that collects movie ratings and makes them available for public download at `https://grouplens.org/datasets/movielens/`. For the purposes of this case study, we have transformed the individual *movies* and *ratings* datasets into a single pivot table where the 300 rows represent 300 different users, and the 3,000 columns represent 3,000 different movies. This transformed, pipe-delimited dataset can be found in the GitHub repository accompanying this book, and is called `movie-ratings-data/user-movie-ratings.csv`.

A sample of the historic user-community movie ratings dataset that we will study looks as follows:

	Movie #1 Toy Story	Movie #2 Monsters Inc.	Movie #3 Saw	Movie #4 Ring	Movie #5 Hitch
User #1	4	5	1	NULL	4
User #2	5	NULL	1	1	NULL
User #3	5	4	3	NULL	3
User #4	5	4	1	1	NULL
User #5	5	5	NULL	NULL	3

In this case, each movie is a different feature (or dimension), and each different user is a different instance (or observation). This sample table, therefore, represents a dataset containing 5 features. However, our actual dataset contains 3,000 different movies, and therefore 3,000 features/dimensions. Furthermore, in a real-life representation, not all users would have rated all the movies, and so there will be a significant number of missing values. Such a dataset, and the matrix used to represent it, is described as *sparse*. These issues would pose a problem for machine learning algorithms, both in terms of computational complexity and the likelihood of over fitting.

To solve this problem, take a closer look at the previous sample table. It seems that users that rated Movie #1 highly (Toy Story) generally also rated Movie #2 highly (Monsters Inc.) as well. We could say, for example, that User #1 is *representative* of all fans of computer-animated children's films, and so we could recommend to User #2 the other movies that User #1 has historically rated highly (this type of recommendation system where we use data from other users is called **collaborative filtering**). At a high level, this is what PCA does—it identifies *typical representations*, called **principal components**, within a high-dimensional dataset so that the dimensions of the original dataset can be reduced while preserving its underlying structure and still be representative in *lower* dimensions! These reduced datasets can then be fed into machine learning models to make predictions as normal, without the fear of any adverse effects from reducing the raw size of the original dataset. Our formal definition of PCA can therefore now be extended so that we can define PCA as the identification of a linear subspace of lower dimensionality where the largest variance in the original dataset is maintained.

Returning to our historic user-community movie ratings dataset, instead of eliminating Movie #2 entirely, we could seek to create a new feature that combines Movie #1 and Movie #2 in some manner. Extending this concept, we can create new features where each new feature is based on all the old features, and thereafter order these new features by how well they help us in predicting user movie ratings. Once ordered, we can drop the least important ones, thereby resulting in a reduction in dimensionality. So how does PCA achieve this? It does so by performing the following steps:

1. First, we standardize the original high-dimensional dataset.
2. Next, we take the standardized data and compute a covariance matrix that provides a means to measure how all our features relate to each other.
3. After computing the covariance matrix, we then find its *eigenvectors* and corresponding *eigenvalues*. Eigenvectors represent the principal components and provide a means to understand the direction of the data. Corresponding eigenvalues represent how much variance there is in the data in that direction.

4. The eigenvectors are then sorted in descending order based on their corresponding eigenvalues, after which the top k eigenvectors are selected representing the most important representations found in the data.

5. A new matrix is then constructed with these k eigenvectors, thereby reducing the original n-dimensional dataset into reduced k dimensions.

Covariance matrix

In mathematics, **variance** refers to a measure of how spread out a dataset is, and is calculated by the sum of the squared distances of each data point, x_i, from the mean *x-bar*, divided by the total number of data points, N. This is represented by the following formula:

$$var(x) = \frac{\sum(x_i - \bar{x})^2}{N}$$

Covariance refers to a measure of how strong the correlation between two or more random variables is (in our case, our independent variables), and is calculated for variables x and y over i dimensions, as follows:

$$cov(x, y) = \frac{\sum(x_i - \bar{x})(y_i - \bar{y})}{N}$$

If the covariance is positive, this implies that the independent variables are positively correlated. If the covariance is negative, this implies that the independent variables are negatively correlated. Finally, a covariance of zero implies that there is no correlation between the independent variables. You may note that we described correlation in Chapter 4, *Supervised Learning Using Apache Spark*, when discussing multivariate linear regression. At that time, we computed the one-way covariance mapping between the dependent variable to all its independent variables. Now we are computing the covariance between all variables.

A **covariance matrix** is a symmetric square matrix where the general element (i, j) is the covariance, *cov(i, j)*, between independent variables i and j (which is the same as the symmetric covariance between j and i). Note that the diagonal in a covariance matrix actually represents just the *variance* between those elements, by definition.

The covariance matrix is shown in the following table:

	x	**y**	**z**
x	var(x)	cov(x, y)	cov(x, z)
y	cov(y, x)	var(y)	cov(y, z)
z	cov(z, x)	cov(z, y)	var(z)

Identity matrix

An identity matrix is a square matrix in which all the elements along the main diagonal are 1 and the remaining elements are 0. Identity matrices are important for when we need to find all of the eigenvectors for a matrix. For example, a 3 x 3 identity matrix looks as follows:

$$\begin{pmatrix} 1 & 0 & 0 \\ 0 & 1 & 0 \\ 0 & 0 & 1 \end{pmatrix}$$

Eigenvectors and eigenvalues

In linear algebra, eigenvectors are a special set of vectors whose *direction* remains unchanged when a linear transformation is applied to it, and only changes by a *scalar* factor. In the context of dimensionality reduction, eigenvectors represent the principal components and provide a means to understand the direction of the data.

Consider a matrix, A, of dimensions (m x n). We can multiply A by a vector, x (of dimensions n x 1 by definition), which results in a new vector, b (of dimensions m x 1), as follows:

$$Ax = \begin{bmatrix} a_{11} & a_{12} & \cdots & a_{1n} \\ a_{21} & a_{22} & \cdots & a_{2n} \\ \vdots & \vdots & \ddots & \vdots \\ a_{m1} & a_{m2} & \cdots & a_{mn} \end{bmatrix} \begin{bmatrix} x_1 \\ x_2 \\ \vdots \\ x_n \end{bmatrix} = \begin{bmatrix} a_{11}x_1 + a_{12}x_2 + \cdots + a_{1n}x_n \\ a_{21}x_1 + a_{22}x_2 + \cdots + a_{2n}x_n \\ \vdots \\ a_{m1}x_1 + a_{m2}x_2 + \cdots + a_{mn}x_n \end{bmatrix}$$

In other words, $Ax = b$.

However, in some cases, the resulting vector, b, is actually a scaled version of the original vector, x. We call this scalar factor λ, in which case the formula above can be rewritten as follows:

$$Ax = \lambda x$$

We say that λ is an *eigenvalue* of matrix A, and x is an *eigenvector* associated with λ. In the context of dimensionality reduction, eigenvalues represent how much variance there is in the data in that direction.

In order to find all the eigenvectors for a matrix, we need to solve the following equation for each eigenvalue, where I is an identity matrix with the same dimensions as matrix A:

$$(A - \lambda I)x = 0$$

The process by which to solve this equation is beyond the scope of this book. However, to learn more about eigenvectors and eigenvalues, please visit `https://en.wikipedia.org/wiki/Eigenvalues_and_eigenvectors`.

Once all of the eigenvectors for the covariance matrix are found, these are then sorted in descending order by their corresponding eigenvalues. Since eigenvalues represent the amount of variance in the data for that direction, the first eigenvector in the ordered list represents the principal component that captures the most variance in the original variables from the original dataset, and so on. For example, as illustrated in *Figure 5.9*, if we were to plot a dataset with two dimensions or features, the first eigenvector (which will be the first principal component in order of importance) would represent the direction of most variation between the two features.

The second eigenvector (the second principal component in order of importance) would represent the direction of second-most variation between the two features:

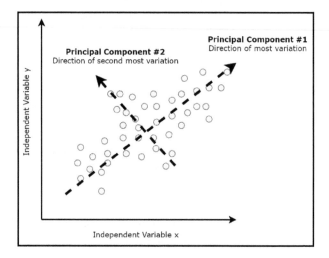

Figure 5.9: Principal components across two dimensions

To help choose the number of principal components, k, to select from the top of the ordered list of eigenvectors, we can plot the number of principal components on the x axis against the cumulative explained variance on the y axis, as illustrated in *Figure 5.10*, where the explained variance is the ratio between the variance of that principal component and the total variance (that is, the sum of all eigenvalues):

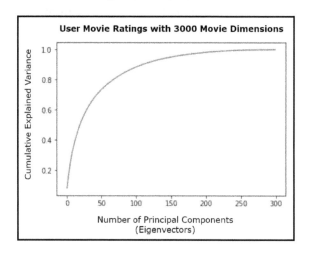

Figure 5.10: Cumulative explained variance

Using *Figure 5.10* as an example, we would select around the first 300 principal components, as these describe the most variation within the data out of the 3,000 in total. Finally, we construct a new matrix by projecting the original dataset into *k*-dimensional space represented by the eigenvectors selected, thereby reducing the dimensionality of the original dataset from 3,000 dimensions to 300 dimensions. This preprocessed and reduced dataset can then be used to train machine learning models as normal.

PCA in Apache Spark

Let's now return to our transformed pipe-delimited user-community movie ratings dataset, `movie-ratings-data/user-movie-ratings.csv`, which contains ratings by 300 users covering 3,000 movies. We will develop an application in Apache Spark that seeks to reduce the dimensionality of this dataset while preserving its structure using PCA. To do this, we will go through the following steps:

 The following subsections describe each of the pertinent cells in the corresponding Jupyter notebook for this use case, called `chp05-02-principal-component-analysis.ipynb`. This can be found in the GitHub repository accompanying this book.

1. First, let's load the transformed, pipe-delimited user-community movie ratings dataset into a Spark dataframe using the following code. The resulting Spark dataframe will have 300 rows (representing the 300 different users) and 3,001 columns (representing the 3,000 different movies plus the user ID column):

```
user_movie_ratings_df = sqlContext.read
    .format('com.databricks.spark.csv').options(header = 'true',
    inferschema = 'true', delimiter = '|')
    .load('<Path to CSV File>')
print((user_movie_ratings_df.count(),
    len(user_movie_ratings_df.columns)))
```

2. We can now generate `MLlib` feature vectors containing 3,000 elements (representing the 3,000 features) using `MLlib`'s `VectorAssembler`, as we have seen before. We can achieve this using the following code:

```
feature_columns = user_movie_ratings_df.columns
feature_columns.remove('userId')
vector_assembler = VectorAssembler(inputCols = feature_columns,
    outputCol = 'features')
user_movie_ratings_features_df = vector_assembler
    .transform(user_movie_ratings_df)
    .select(['userId', 'features'])
```

3. Before we can reduce the dimensionality of the dataset using PCA, we first need to standardize the features that we described previously. This can be achieved using MLlib's StandardScaler estimator and fitting it to the Spark dataframe containing our feature vectors, as follows:

```
standardizer = StandardScaler(withMean=True, withStd=True,
    inputCol='features', outputCol='std_features')
standardizer_model = standardizer
    .fit(user_movie_ratings_features_df)
user_movie_ratings_standardized_features_df =
    standardizer_model.transform(user_movie_ratings_features_df)
```

4. Next, we convert our scaled features into a MLlib RowMatrix instance. A RowMatrix is a distributed matrix with no index, where each row is a vector. We achieve this by converting our scaled features data frame into an RDD and mapping each row of the RDD to the corresponding scaled feature vector. We then pass this RDD to MLlib's RowMatrix() (as shown in the following code), resulting in a matrix of standardized feature vectors of dimensions 300 x 3,000:

```
scaled_features_rows_rdd =
    user_movie_ratings_standardized_features_df
    .select("std_features").rdd
scaled_features_matrix = RowMatrix(scaled_features_rows_rdd
    .map(lambda x: x[0].tolist()))
```

5. Now that we have our standardized data in matrix form, we can easily compute the top *k* principal components by invoking the computePrincipalComponents() method exposed by MLlib's RowMatrix. We can compute the top 300 principal components as follows:

```
number_principal_components = 300
principal_components = scaled_features_matrix
    .computePrincipalComponents(number_principal_components)
```

6. Now that we have identified the top 300 principal components, we can project the standardized user-community movie ratings data from 3,000 dimensions to a linear subspace of only 300 dimensions while preserving the largest variances from the original dataset. This is achieved by using matrix multiplication and multiplying the matrix containing the standardized data by the matrix containing the top 300 principal components, as follows:

```
projected_matrix = scaled_features_matrix
    .multiply(principal_components)
print((projected_matrix.numRows(), projected_matrix.numCols()))
```

The resulting matrix now has dimensions of 300 x 300, confirming the reduction in dimensionality from the original 3,000 to only 300! We can now use this projected matrix and its PCA feature vectors as the input into subsequent machine learning models as normal.

7. Alternatively, we can use `MLlib`'s `PCA()` estimator directly on the dataframe containing our standardized feature vectors to generate a new dataframe with a new column containing the PCA feature vectors, as follows:

```
pca = PCA(k=number_principal_components, inputCol="std_features",
    outputCol="pca_features")
pca_model = pca.fit(user_movie_ratings_standardized_features_df)
user_movie_ratings_pca_df = pca_model
    .transform(user_movie_ratings_standardized_features_df)
```

Again, this new dataframe and its PCA feature vectors can then be used to train subsequent machine learning models as normal.

8. Finally, we can extract the explained variance for each principal component from our PCA model by accessing its `explainedVariance` attribute as follows:

```
pca_model.explainedVariance
```

The resulting vector (of 300 elements) shows that, in our example, the first eigenvector (and therefore the first principal component) in the ordered list of principal components explains 8.2% of the variance, the second explains 4%, and so on.

In this case study, we have demonstrated how we can reduce the dimensionality of the user-community movie ratings dataset from 3,000 dimensions to only 300 dimensions while preserving its structure using PCA. The resulting reduced dataset can then be used to train machine learning models as normal, such as a hierarchical clustering model for collaborative filtering.

Summary

In this chapter, we have trained and evaluated various unsupervised machine learning models and techniques in Apache Spark using a variety of real-world use cases, including partitioning the various substances found in the human brain using image segmentation and helping to develop a movie recommendation system by reducing the dimensionality of a high-dimensional user-community movie ratings dataset.

In the next chapter, we will develop, test, and evaluate some common algorithms that are used in **natural language processing** (**NLP**) in an attempt to train machines to automatically analyze and understand human text and speech!

6
Natural Language Processing Using Apache Spark

In this chapter, we'll study and implement common algorithms that are used in NLP, which can help us develop machines that are capable of automatically analyzing and understanding human text and speech in context. Specifically, we will study and implement the following classes of computer science algorithms related to NLP:

- Feature transformers, including the following:
  - Tokenization
  - Stemming
  - Lemmatization
  - Normalization
- Feature extractors, including the following :
  - Bag of words
  - Term frequency–inverse document frequency

Feature transformers

The fundamental concept behind natural language processing is treating human text and speech as data—just like the structured and unstructured numerical and categorical data sources we have encountered in this book thus far—while preserving its *context*. However, natural language is notoriously difficult to understand, even for humans, let alone machines! Not only does natural language consist of hundreds of different spoken languages, with different writing systems, but it also poses other challenges, such as different tones, inflections, slang, abbreviations, metaphors, and sarcasm. Writing systems and communication platforms in particular provide us with text that may contain spelling mistakes, unconventional grammar, and sentences that are loosely structured.

Our first challenge, therefore, is to convert natural language into data that can be used by a machine while preserving its underlying context. Furthermore, when applied to machine learning, we also need to convert natural language into feature vectors in order to train machine learning models. Well, there are two broad classes of computer science algorithms that help us with these challenges—**feature extractors**, which help us extract relevant features from the natural language data, and **feature transformers**, which help us scale, convert, and/or modify these features in preparation for subsequent modelling. In this subsection, we will discuss feature transformers and how they can help us convert our natural language data into structures that are easier to process. First, let's introduce some common definitions within NLP.

Document

In NLP, a document represents a logical container of text. The container itself can be anything that makes sense within the context of your use case. For example, one document could refer to a single article, record, social media posting, or tweet.

Corpus

Once you have defined what your document represents, a corpus is defined as a logical collection of documents. Using the previous examples, a corpus could represent a collection of articles (for example, a magazine or blog) or a collection of tweets (for example, tweets with a particular hashtag).

Preprocessing pipeline

One of the basic tasks involved in NLP is the preprocessing of your documents in an attempt to standardize the text from different sources as much as possible. Not only does preprocessing help us to standardize text, it often reduces the size of the raw text, thereby reducing the computational complexity of subsequent processes and models. The following subsections describe common preprocessing techniques that may constitute a typical ordered preprocessing pipeline.

Tokenization

Tokenization refers to the technique of splitting up your text into individual *tokens* or terms. Formally, a token is defined as a sequence of characters that represents a subset of the original text. Informally, tokens are typically just the different words that make up the original text, and that have been segmented using the whitespace and other punctuation characters. For example, the sentence "Machine Learning with Apache Spark" may result in a collection of tokens persisted in an array or list expressed as `["Machine", "Learning", "with", "Apache", "Spark"]`.

Stop words

Stop words are common words in a given language that are used to structure a sentence grammatically, but that are not necessarily helpful in determining its underlying meaning or sentiment. For example, in the English language, common stop words include *and, I, there, this,* and *with*. A common preprocessing technique is to therefore remove these words from the collection of tokens by filtering based on a language-specific lookup of stop words. Using our previous example, our filtered list of tokens would be `["Machine", "Learning", "Apache", "Spark]`.

Stemming

Stemming refers to the technique of reducing words to a common base or *stem*. For example, the words "connection", "connections", "connective", "connected", and "connecting" can all be reduced to their common stem of "connect". Stemming is not a perfect process, and stemming algorithms are liable to make mistakes. However, for the purposes of reducing the size of a dataset in order to train a machine learning model, it is a valuable technique. Using our previous example, our filtered list of stems would be `["Machin", "Learn", "Apach", "Spark"]`.

Lemmatization

While stemming quickly reduces words to a base form, it does not take into account the context, and can therefore not differentiate between words that have different meanings depending on their position within a sentence or context. Lemmatization does not crudely reduce words purely based on a common stem, but instead aims to remove inflectional endings only in order to return a dictionary form of a word called its *lemma*. For example, the words *am, is, being,* and *was* can be reduced to the lemma *be,* while a stemmer would not be able to infer this contextual meaning.

While lemmatization can be used to preserve context and meaning to a better extent, it comes at the cost of additional computational complexity and processing time. Using our previous example, our filtered list of lemmas may therefore look like `["Machine"`, `"Learning"`, `"Apache"`, `"Spark"]`.

Normalization

Finally, normalization refers to a wide variety of common techniques that are used to standardize text. Typical normalization techniques include converting all text to lowercase, removing selected characters, punctuation and other sequences of characters (typically using regular expressions), and expanding abbreviations by applying language-specific dictionaries of common abbreviations and slang terms.

Figure 6.1 illustrates a typical ordered preprocessing pipeline that is used to standardize raw written text:

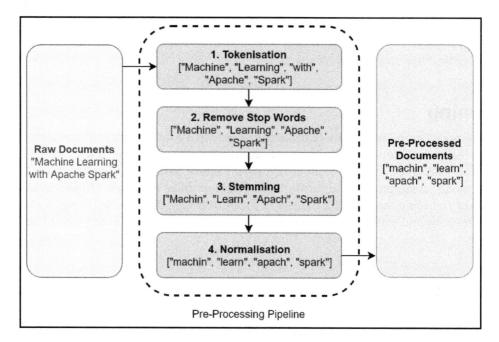

Figure 6.1: Typical preprocessing pipeline

Feature extractors

We have seen how feature transformers allow us to convert, modify, and standardize our documents using a preprocessing pipeline, resulting in the conversion of raw text into a collection of tokens. *Feature extractors* take these tokens and generate feature vectors from them that may then be used to train machine learning models. Two common examples of typical feature extractors that are used in NLP are the **bag of words** and **term frequency–inverse document frequency (TF–IDF)** algorithms.

Bag of words

The *bag of words* approach simply counts the number of occurrences of each unique word in the raw or tokenized text. For example, given the text "Machine Learning with Apache Spark, Apache Spark's MLlib and Apache Kafka", the bag of words approach would provide us with the following numerical feature vector:

Machine	Learning	with	Apache	Spark	MLlib	Kafka
1	1	1	3	2	1	1

Note that each unique word is a feature or dimension, and that the bag of words approach is a simple technique that is often employed as a baseline model with which to compare the performance of more advanced feature extractors.

Term frequency–inverse document frequency

TF–IDF aims to improve upon the bag of words approach by providing an indication of how *important* each word is, taking into account how often that word appears across the entire corpus.

Let us use *TF(t, d)* to denote the **term frequency**, which is the number of times that a term, *t*, appears in a document, *d*. Let's also use *DF(t, D)* to denote the **document frequency**, which is the number of documents in our corpus, *D*, that contain the term *t*. We can then define the **inverse document frequency** *IDF(t, D)* as follows:

$$IDF(t, D) = log\frac{|D|+1}{DF(t,D)+1}$$

The IDF provides us with a measure of how important a term is, taking into account how often that term appears across the entire corpus, where $|D|$ is the total number of documents in our corpus, D. Terms that are less common across the corpus have a higher IDF metric. Note, however, that because of the use of the logarithm, if a term appears in all documents, its IDF becomes 0—that is, *log(1)*. IDF, therefore, provides a metric whereby more value is placed on rarer terms that are important in describing documents.

Finally, to calculate the TF–IDF measure, we simply multiply the term frequency by the inverse document frequency as follows:

$$TFIDF(t, d, D) = TF(t, d) \cdot IDF(t, D)$$

This implies that the TF–IDF measure increases proportionally with the number of times that a word appears in a document, offset by the frequency of the word across the entire corpus. This is important because the term frequency alone may highlight words such as "a", "I", and "the" that appear very often in a given document but that do not help us determine the underlying meaning or sentiment of the text. By employing TF–IDF, we can reduce the impact of these types of words on our analysis.

Case study – sentiment analysis

Let's now apply these feature transformers and feature extractors to a very modern real-world use case—sentiment analysis. In sentiment analysis, the goal is to classify the underlying human sentiment—for example, whether the writer is positive, neutral, or negative towards the subject of a text. To many organizations, sentiment analysis is an important technique that is used to better understand their customers and target markets. For example, sentiment analysis can be used by retailers to gauge the public's reaction to a particular product, or by politicians to assess public mood towards a policy or news item. In our case study, we will examine tweets about airlines in order to predict whether customers are saying positive or negative things about them. Our analysis could then be used by airlines in order to improve their customer service by focusing on those tweets that have been classified as negative in sentiment.

The corpus of tweets that we will use for our case study has been downloaded from **Figure Eight**, a company that provides businesses with high-quality training datasets for real-world machine learning. Figure Eight also provides a Data for Everyone platform containing open datasets that are available for download by the public, and which may be found at https://www.figure-eight.com/data-for-everyone/.

If you open `twitter-data/airline-tweets-labelled-corpus.csv` in any text editor from either the GitHub repository accompanying this book or from Figure Eight's Data for Everyone platform, you will find a collection of 14,872 tweets about major airlines that were scraped from Twitter in February 2015. These tweets have also been pre-labelled for us, with a sentiment classification of positive, negative, or neutral. The pertinent columns in this dataset are described in the following table:

Column Name	Data Type	Description
unit_id	Long	Unique identifier (primary key)
airline_sentiment	String	Sentiment classification—positive, neutral, or negative
airline	String	Name of the airline
text	String	Textual content of the tweet

Our goal will be to use this corpus of tweets in order to train a machine learning model to predict whether future tweets about a given airline are positive or negative in sentiment towards that airline.

NLP pipeline

Before we look at the Python code for our case study, let's visualize the end-to-end NLP pipeline that we will construct. Our NLP pipeline for this case study is illustrated in *Figure 6.2*:

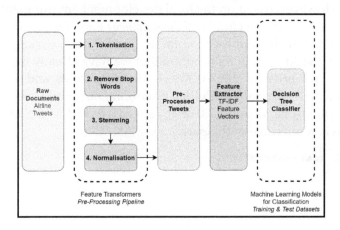

Figure 6.2: End-to-end NLP pipeline

NLP in Apache Spark

As of Spark 2.3.2, tokenization and stop-word removal feature transformers (among a wide variety of others), and the TF–IDF feature extractor is available natively in MLlib. Although stemming, lemmatization, and standardization can be achieved indirectly through transformations on Spark dataframes in Spark 2.3.2 (via **user-defined functions (UDFs)** and map functions that are applied to RDDs), we will be using a third-party Spark library called spark-nlp to perform these feature transformations. This third-party library has been designed to extend the features already available in MLlib by providing an easy-to-use API for distributed NLP annotations on Spark dataframes at scale. To learn more about spark-nlp, please visit https://nlp.johnsnowlabs.com/. Finally, we will use the estimators and transformers that are already available natively in MLlib—as we have seen in previous chapters—to train our final machine learning classification models.

Note that by using feature transformers and extractors native to MLlib followed by feature transformers provided by the third-party spark-nlp library, before finally applying native MLlib estimators, we will be required to explicitly define and develop data transformation stages in our pipeline in order to conform to the underlying data structures expected by the two different libraries. While this is not recommended for production-grade pipelines because of its inefficiencies, one of the purposes of this section is to demonstrate how to use both libraries for NLP. Readers will then be in an informed position to choose a suitable library, depending on the requirements of the use case in question.

Depending on your environment setup, there are a few methods that are available that can be used to install spark-nlp, as described at https://nlp.johnsnowlabs.com/quickstart.html. However, based on the local development environment that we provisioned in Chapter 2, *Setting Up a Local Development Environment*, we will install spark-nlp using pip, which is another commonly used Python package manager that comes bundled with the Anaconda distribution that we have already installed (at the time of writing, spark-nlp is not available via the conda repositories, and so we shall use pip instead). To install spark-nlp for our Python environment, simply execute the following command, which will install version 1.7.0 of spark-nlp (which is the latest version as of writing, and which is compatible with Spark 2.x):

```
> pip install spark-nlp==1.7.0
```

We then need to tell Spark where it can find the `spark-nlp` library. We can do this either by defining an additional parameter in `{SPARK_HOME}/conf/spark-defaults.conf` or by setting the `spark.jars` configuration within our code when instantiating a Spark context, as follows:

```
conf = SparkConf().set("spark.jars",
'/opt/anaconda3/lib/python3.6/sitepackages/sparknlp/lib/sparknlp.jar')
    .setAppName("Natural Language Processing - Sentiment Analysis")
sc = SparkContext(conf=conf)
```

Please refer to `Chapter 2`, *Setting Up a Local Development Environment*, for further details regarding defining the configuration for Apache Spark. Note that in a multinode Spark cluster, all third-party Python packages either need to be installed on all Spark nodes or your Spark application itself needs to be packaged into a self-contained file containing all third-party dependencies. This self-contained file is then distributed to all nodes in the Spark cluster.

We are now ready to develop our NLP pipeline in Apache Spark in order to perform sentiment analysis on our corpus of airline tweets! Let's go through the following steps:

> The following subsections describe each of the pertinent cells in the corresponding Jupyter notebook for this use case, called `chp06-01-natural-language-processing.ipynb`. It can be found in the GitHub repository accompanying this book.

1. As well as importing the standard PySpark dependencies, we also need to import the relevant `spark-nlp` dependencies, including its `Tokenizer`, `Stemmer`, and `Normalizer` classes, as follows:

```
import findspark
findspark.init()
from pyspark import SparkContext, SparkConf
from pyspark.sql import SQLContext
from pyspark.sql.functions import *
from pyspark.sql.types import StructType, StructField
from pyspark.sql.types import LongType, DoubleType, IntegerType,
StringType, BooleanType
from pyspark.ml.feature import VectorAssembler
from pyspark.ml.feature import StringIndexer
from pyspark.ml.feature import Tokenizer
from pyspark.ml.feature import StopWordsRemover
from pyspark.ml.feature import HashingTF, IDF
from pyspark.ml import Pipeline, PipelineModel
from pyspark.ml.classification import DecisionTreeClassifier
from pyspark.ml.evaluation import BinaryClassificationEvaluator
```

```
from pyspark.mllib.evaluation import MulticlassMetrics

from sparknlp.base import *
from sparknlp.annotator import Tokenizer as NLPTokenizer
from sparknlp.annotator import Stemmer, Normalizer
```

2. Next, we instantiate a `SparkContext` as usual. Note, however, that in this case, we explicitly tell Spark where to find the `spark-nlp` library using the `spark-jars` configuration parameter. We can then invoke the `getConf()` method on our `SparkContext` instance to review the current Spark configuration, as follows:

```
conf = SparkConf().set("spark.jars",
'/opt/anaconda3/lib/python3.6/site-
packages/sparknlp/lib/sparknlp.jar')
    .setAppName("Natural Language Processing - Sentiment Analysis")
sc = SparkContext(conf=conf)
sqlContext = SQLContext(sc)
sc.getConf().getAll()
```

3. After loading our corpus of airline tweets from `twitter-data/airline-tweets-labelled-corpus.csv` into a Spark dataframe called `airline_tweets_df`, we generate a new label column. The existing dataset already contains a label column called `airline_sentiment`, which is either `"positive"`, `"neutral"`, or `"negative"` based on a manual pre-classification. Although positive messages are naturally always welcome, in reality, the most useful messages are usually the negative ones. By automatically identifying and studying the negative messages, organizations can focus more efficiently on how to improve their products and services based on negative feedback. Therefore, we will create a new label column called `negative_sentiment_label` that is `"true"` if the underlying sentiment has been classified as `"negative"` and `"false"` otherwise, as shown in the following code:

```
airline_tweets_with_labels_df = airline_tweets_df
    .withColumn("negative_sentiment_label",
        when(col("airline_sentiment") == "negative", lit("true"))
        .otherwise(lit("false")))
    .select("unit_id", "text", "negative_sentiment_label")
```

4. We are now ready to build and apply our preprocessing pipeline to our corpus of raw tweets! Here, we demonstrate how to utilize the feature transformers native to Spark's `MLlib`, namely its `Tokenizer` and `StopWordsRemover` transformers. First, we tokenize the raw textual content of each tweet using the `Tokenizer` transformer, resulting in a new column containing a list of parsed tokens. We then pass this column containing the tokens to the `StopWordsRemover` transformer, which removes English language (default) stop words from this list, resulting in a new column containing the list of filtered tokens. In the next cell, we will demonstrate how to utilize the feature transformers available in the `spark-nlp` third-party library. However, `spark-nlp` requires a column of a `string` type as its initial input, not a list of tokens. Therefore, the final statement concatenates the list of filtered tokens back into a whitespace-delimited `string` column, as follows:

```
filtered_df = airline_tweets_with_labels_df
    .filter("text is not null")
tokenizer = Tokenizer(inputCol="text", outputCol="tokens_1")
tokenized_df = tokenizer.transform(filtered_df)
remover = StopWordsRemover(inputCol="tokens_1",
    outputCol="filtered_tokens")
preprocessed_part_1_df = remover.transform(tokenized_df)
preprocessed_part_1_df = preprocessed_part_1_df
    .withColumn("concatenated_filtered_tokens",
        concat_ws(" ", col("filtered_tokens")))
```

5. We can now demonstrate how to utilize the feature transformers and annotators available in the `spark-nlp` third-party library, namely its `DocumentAssembler` transformer and `Tokenizer`, `Stemmer`, and `Normalizer` annotators. First, we create annotated documents from our string column that are required as the initial input into the `spark-nlp` pipelines. Then, we apply the `spark-nlp Tokenizer` and `Stemmer` annotators to convert our filtered list of tokens into a list of *stems*. Finally, we apply its `Normalizer` annotator, which converts the stems into lowercase by default. All of these stages are defined within a *pipeline*, which, as we saw in `Chapter 4`, *Supervised Learning Using Apache Spark,* is an ordered list of machine learning and data transformation steps that is executed on a Spark dataframe.

We execute our pipeline on our dataset, resulting in a new dataframe called `preprocessed_df` from which we keep only the relevant columns that are required for subsequent analysis and modelling, namely `unit_id` (unique record identifier), `text` (original raw textual content of the tweet), `negative_sentiment_label` (our new label), and `normalised_stems` (a `spark-nlp` array of filtered, stemmed, and normalized tokens as a result of our preprocessing pipeline), as shown in the following code:

```
document_assembler = DocumentAssembler()
    .setInputCol("concatenated_filtered_tokens")
tokenizer = NLPTokenizer()
    .setInputCols(["document"]).setOutputCol("tokens_2")
stemmer = Stemmer().setInputCols(["tokens_2"])
    .setOutputCol("stems")
normalizer = Normalizer()
    .setInputCols(["stems"]).setOutputCol("normalised_stems")
pipeline = Pipeline(stages=[document_assembler, tokenizer, stemmer,
    normalizer])
pipeline_model = pipeline.fit(preprocessed_part_1_df)
preprocessed_df = pipeline_model.transform(preprocessed_part_1_df)
preprocessed_df.select("unit_id", "text",
    "negative_sentiment_label", "normalised_stems")
```

6. Before we can create feature vectors from our array of stemmed tokens using `MLlib`'s native feature extractors, there is one final preprocessing step. The column containing our stemmed tokens, namely `normalised_stems`, persists these tokens in a specialized `spark-nlp` array structure. We need to convert this `spark-nlp` array back into a standard list of tokens so that we may apply `MLlib`'s native TF–IDF algorithms to it. We achieve this by first exploding the `spark-nlp` array structure, which has the effect of creating a new dataframe observation for every element in this array. We then group our Spark dataframe by `unit_id`, which is the primary key for each unique tweet, before aggregating the stems using the whitespace delimiter into a new string column called `tokens`. Finally, we apply the `split` function to this column to convert the aggregated string into a list of strings or tokens, as shown in the following code:

```
exploded_df = preprocessed_df
    .withColumn("stems", explode("normalised_stems"))
    .withColumn("stems", col("stems").getItem("result"))
    .select("unit_id", "negative_sentiment_label", "text", "stems")

aggregated_df = exploded_df.groupBy("unit_id")
    .agg(concat_ws(" ", collect_list(col("stems"))),
        first("text"), first("negative_sentiment_label"))
```

```
      .toDF("unit_id", "tokens", "text", "negative_sentiment_label")
    .withColumn("tokens", split(col("tokens"), " ")
       .cast("array<string>"))
```

7. We are now ready to generate feature vectors from our list of filtered, stemmed, and normalized tokens! As discussed, we will be using the TF–IDF feature extractor to generate feature vectors rather than the basic bag of words approach. The TF–IDF feature extractor is native to `MLlib` and comes in two parts. First, we generate the **term frequency (TF)** feature vectors by passing our list of tokens into `MLlib`'s `HashingTF` transformer. We then *fit* `MLlib`'s **inverse document frequency (IDF)** estimator to our dataframe containing the term frequency feature vectors, as shown in the following code. The result is a new Spark dataframe with our TF–IDF feature vectors contained in a column called `features`:

```
hashingTF = HashingTF(inputCol="tokens", outputCol="raw_features",
    numFeatures=280)
features_df = hashingTF.transform(aggregated_df)
idf = IDF(inputCol="raw_features", outputCol="features")
idf_model = idf.fit(features_df)
scaled_features_df = idf_model.transform(features_df)
```

8. As we saw in `Chapter 4`, *Supervised Learning Using Apache Spark*, since our label column is categorical in nature, we need to apply `MLlib`'s `StringIndexer` to it in order to identify and index all possible classifications. The result is a new Spark dataframe with an indexed label column called `"label"`, which is 0.0 if `negative_sentiment_label` is `true`, and 1.0 if `negative_sentiment_label` is `false`, as shown in the following code:

```
indexer = StringIndexer(inputCol = "negative_sentiment_label",
    outputCol = "label").fit(scaled_features_df)
scaled_features_indexed_label_df =
indexer.transform(scaled_features_df)
```

9. We are now ready to create training and test dataframes in order to train and evaluate subsequent machine learning models. We achieve this as normal, using the `randomSplit` method (as shown in the following code), but in this case, 90% of all observations will go into our training dataframe, with the remaining 10% going into our test dataframe:

```
train_df, test_df = scaled_features_indexed_label_df
    .randomSplit([0.9, 0.1], seed=12345)
```

10. In this example, we will be training a supervised decision tree classifier (see `Chapter 4`, *Supervised Learning Using Apache Spark*) in order to help us classify whether a given tweet is positive or negative in sentiment. As in `Chapter 4`, *Supervised Learning Using Apache Spark*, we fit `MLlib`'s `DecisionTreeClassifier` estimator to our training dataframe in order to train our classification tree, as shown in the following code:

```
decision_tree = DecisionTreeClassifier(featuresCol = 'features',
    labelCol = 'label')
decision_tree_model = decision_tree.fit(train_df)
```

11. Now that we have a trained classification tree, we can apply it to our test dataframe in order to classify test tweets. As we did in `Chapter 4`, *Supervised Learning Using Apache Spark*, we apply our trained classification tree to the test dataframe using the `transform()` method (as shown in the following code), and afterwards study its predicted classifications:

```
test_decision_tree_predictions_df = decision_tree_model
    .transform(test_df)
print("TEST DATASET PREDICTIONS AGAINST ACTUAL LABEL: ")
test_decision_tree_predictions_df.select("prediction", "label",
    "text").show(10, False)
```

For example, our decision tree classifier has predicted that the following tweets from our test dataframe are negative in sentiment:

- "I need you...to be a better airline. ^LOL"
- "if you can't guarantee parents will sit with their children, don't sell tickets with that promise"
- "resolved and im sick and tired of waiting on you. I want my refund and I'd like to speak to someone about it."
- "I would have loved to respond to your website until I saw the really long form. In business the new seats are bad"

A human would also probably classify these tweets as negative in sentiment! But more importantly, airlines can use this model and the tweets that it identifies to focus on areas for improvement. Based on this sample of tweets, such areas would include website usability, ticket marketing, and the time taken to process refunds.

12. Finally, in order to quantify the accuracy of our trained classification tree, let's compute its confusion matrix on the test data using the following code:

```
predictions_and_label = test_decision_tree_predictions_df
    .select("prediction", "label").rdd
metrics = MulticlassMetrics(predictions_and_label)
print("N = %g" % test_decision_tree_predictions_df.count())
print(metrics.confusionMatrix())
```

The resulting confusion matrix looks as follows:

	Predict $y = 0$ (Negative)	Predict $y = 1$ (Non-Negative)
Actual $y = 0$ (Negative)	725	209
Actual $y = 1$ (Non-Negative)	244	325

We can interpret this confusion matrix as follows—out of a total of 1,503 test tweets, our model exhibits the following properties:

- Correctly classifies 725 tweets as negative in sentiment that are actually negative
- Correctly classifies 325 tweets as non-negative in sentiment that are actually non-negative
- Incorrectly classifies 209 tweets as non-negative in sentiment that are actually negative
- Incorrectly classifies 244 tweets as negative in sentiment that are actually non-negative
- Overall accuracy = 70%
- Overall error rate = 30%
- Sensitivity = 57%
- Specificity = 78%

So, based on a default threshold value of 0.5 (which in this case study is fine because we have no preference over what type of error is better), our decision tree classifier has an overall accuracy rate of 70%, which is quite good!

13. For the sake of completeness, let's train a decision tree classifier, but using the feature vectors that are derived from the bag of words algorithm. Note that we already computed these feature vectors when we applied the `HashingTF` transformer to our preprocessed corpus to calculate the term frequency (TF) feature vectors. Therefore, we can just repeat our machine learning pipeline, but based only on the output of the `HashingTF` transformer instead, as follows:

```
# Create Training and Test DataFrames based on the Bag of Words
Feature Vectors
bow_indexer = StringIndexer(inputCol = "negative_sentiment_label",
    outputCol = "label").fit(features_df)
bow_features_indexed_label_df = bow_indexer.transform(features_df)
    .withColumnRenamed("raw_features", "features")
bow_train_df, bow_test_df = bow_features_indexed_label_df
    .randomSplit([0.9, 0.1], seed=12345)

# Train a Decision Tree Classifier using the Bag of Words Feature
Vectors
bow_decision_tree = DecisionTreeClassifier(featuresCol =
    'features', labelCol = 'label')
bow_decision_tree_model = bow_decision_tree.fit(bow_train_df)

# Apply the Bag of Words Decision Tree Classifier to the Test
DataFrame and generate the Confusion Matrix
bow_test_decision_tree_predictions_df = bow_decision_tree_model
    .transform(bow_test_df)
bow_predictions_and_label = bow_test_decision_tree_predictions_df
    .select("prediction", "label").rdd
bow_metrics = MulticlassMetrics(bow_predictions_and_label)
print("N = %g" % bow_test_decision_tree_predictions_df.count())
print(bow_metrics.confusionMatrix())
```

Note that the resulting confusion matrix is exactly the same as when we applied our decision tree classifier that had been trained on the *scaled* feature vectors using the `IDF` estimator (given the same random split seed and size of the training dataframe). This is because of the fact that our corpus of tweets is relatively small at 14,872 documents, and therefore the effect of scaling the term frequency (TF) feature vectors based on the frequency across the corpus will have a negligible impact on the predictive quality of this specific model.

14. A very useful feature provided by `MLlib` is the ability to save trained machine learning models to disk for later use. We can take advantage of this feature by saving our trained decision tree classifier to the local disk of our single-node development environment. In multi-node clusters, trained models may also be saved to a distributed file system, such as the Apache Hadoop Distributed File system (see `Chapter 1`, *The Big Data Ecosystem*) by simply using the relevant file system prefix (for example `hdfs://<HDFS NameNode URL>/<HDFS Path>`), as shown in the following code:

    ```
    bow_decision_tree_model.save('<Target filesystem path to save MLlib
    Model>')
    ```

 Our trained decision tree classifier for performing sentiment analysis of airline tweets has also been pushed to the GitHub repository accompanying this book, and may be found in `chapter06/models/airline-sentiment-analysis-decision-tree-classifier`.

Summary

In this chapter, we have studied, implemented, and evaluated common algorithms that are used in natural language processing. We have preprocessed a corpus of documents using feature transformers and generated feature vectors from the resulting processed corpus using feature extractors. We have also applied these common NLP algorithms to machine learning. We trained and tested a sentiment analysis model that we used to predict the underlying sentiment of tweets so that organizations may improve their product and service offerings. In `Chapter 8`, *Real-Time Machine Learning Using Apache Spark*, we will extend our sentiment analysis model to operate in real time using Spark Streaming and Apache Kafka.

In the next chapter, we will take a hands-on exploration through the exciting and cutting-edge world of deep learning!

Deep Learning Using Apache Spark

7

In this chapter, we will go on a hands-on exploration of the exciting and cutting-edge world of deep learning! We will use third-party deep learning libraries in conjunction with Apache Spark's `MLlib` to perform accurate **optical character recognition** (**OCR**) and automatically recognize and classify images via the following types of artificial neural networks and machine learning algorithms:

- Multilayer perceptrons
- Convolutional neural networks
- Transfer learning

Artificial neural networks

As we studied in Chapter 3, *Artificial Intelligence and Machine Learning*, an **artificial neural network** (**ANN**) is a connected group of artificial neurons that is aggregated into three types of linked neural layers—the input layer, zero or more hidden layers, and the output layer. A **monolayer** ANN consists of just *one* layer of links between the input nodes and output nodes, while **multilayer** ANNs are characterized by the segmentation of artificial neurons across multiple linked layers.

An ANN where signals are propagated in one direction only—that is, the signals are received by the input layer and forwarded to the next layer for processing—are called **feedforward** networks. ANNs where a signal may be propagated back to artificial neurons or neural layers that have already processed that signal are called **feedback** networks.

Backwards propagation is a supervised learning process by which multilayer ANNs can learn—that is, derive an optimal set of weight coefficients. First, all weights are initially set as random and the output from the network is calculated. If the predicted output does not match the desired output, the total error at the output nodes is propagated back through the entire network in an effort to readjust all weights in the network so that the error is reduced in the output layer. In other words, backwards propagation seeks to minimize the difference between the actual output and the desired output via an iterative weight adjustment process.

Multilayer perceptrons

A **single-layer perceptron** (**SLP**) is a basic type of ANN that consists of just two layers of nodes—an input layer containing input nodes and an output layer containing output nodes. A **multilayer perceptron** (**MLP**), however, introduces one or more hidden layers between the input and output layers, giving them the ability to learn nonlinear functions, as illustrated in *Figure 7.1*:

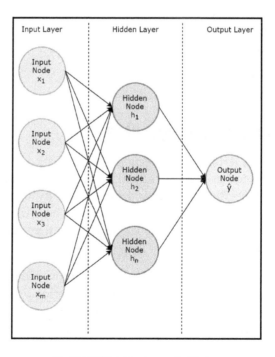

Figure 7.1: Multilayer perceptron neural architecture

MLP classifier

Apache Spark's machine learning library, `MLlib`, provides an out-of-the-box **multilayer perceptron classifier** (**MLPC**) that can be applied to classification problems where we are required to predict from *k* possible classes.

Input layer

In `MLlib`'s MLPC, the nodes in the input layer represent the input data. Let's denote this input data as a vector, *X*, with *m* features, as follows:

$$X : x_1, x_2, \ldots, x_m$$

Hidden layers

The input data is then passed to the hidden layers. For the sake of simplicity, let's say that we have only one hidden layer, h^1, and that within this one hidden layer, we have *n* neurons, as follows:

$$h^1 neurons : h_1^1, h_2^1, \ldots, h_n^1$$

The net input, *z*, into the activation function for each of these hidden neurons is then the input data set vector, *X*, multiplied by a weight set vector, W^n (corresponding to the weight sets assigned to the *n* neurons in the hidden layer), where each weight set vector, W^n, contains *m* weights (corresponding to the *m* features in our input data set vector *X*), as follows:

$$W^n : w_1^n, w_2^n, \ldots, w_m^n$$

In linear algebra, the product of multiplying one vector by another is called the **dot product**, and it outputs a scalar (that is, a number) represented by *z*, as follows:

$$z = W \cdot X = w_1 x_1 + w_2 x_2 + \ldots + w_m x_m = \sum_{i=1}^{m} w_i x_i + bias$$

The **bias**, as illustrated in `Chapter 3`, *Artificial Intelligence and Machine Learning*, and shown in *Figure 3.5*, is a *stand-alone* constant analogous to the intercept term in a regression model, and may be added to non-output layers in feedforward neural networks. It is called standalone because bias nodes are not connected to preceding layers. By introducing a constant, we allow for the output of an activation function to be shifted left or right by that constant, thereby increasing the flexibility of an ANN to learn patterns more effectively by providing the ability to shift decision boundaries based on the data.

Note that in a single hidden layer containing n hidden neurons, n dot product calculations will be computed, as illustrated in *Figure 7.2*:

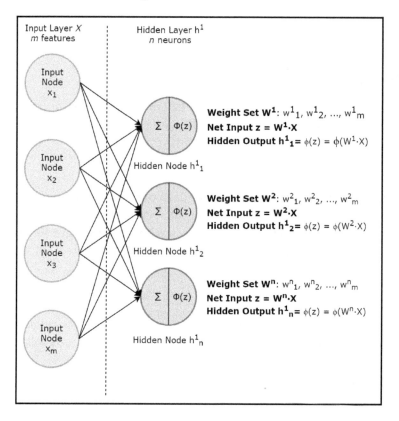

Figure 7.2: Hidden layer net input and output

In `MLlib`'s MLPC, the hidden neurons use the **sigmoid** activation function, as shown in the following formula:

$$\phi(z) = \sigma(z) = \frac{1}{1+e^{-z}}$$

As we saw in `Chapter 3`, *Artificial Intelligence and Machine Learning*, the sigmoid (or logistic) function is bounded between 0 and 1, and is smoothly defined for all real input values. By using the sigmoid activation function, the nodes in the hidden layers actually correspond to a logistic regression model. If we study the sigmoid curve, as shown in *Figure 7.3*, we can state that if the net input, z, is a large positive number, then the output of the sigmoid function, and hence the activation function for our hidden neurons, will be close to 1. Conversely, if the net input, z, is a negative number with a large absolute value, then the output of the sigmoid function will be close to 0:

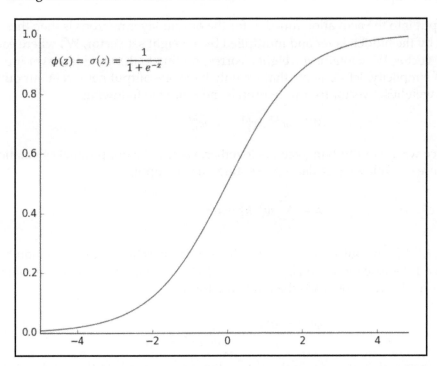

Figure 7.3: Sigmoid function

In all cases, each hidden neuron will take the net input, z, which is the dot product of the input data, X, and the weight set, W^n, plus a bias, and apply that to the sigmoid function, finally outputting a number between 0 and 1. After all hidden neurons have computed the result of their activation function, we will then have n hidden outputs from our hidden layer h^1, as follows:

$$h^1\ outputs : (h^1_1, h^1_2, \ldots, h^1_n)$$

Output layer

The hidden layer outputs are then used as inputs to calculate the final outputs in the output layer. In our case, we only have a single hidden layer, h^1, with outputs $h^1_1, h^1_2, \ldots, h^1_n$. These then become n inputs into the output layer.

The net input into the activation function for the output layer neurons is then these n inputs computed by the hidden layer and multiplied by a weight set vector, W^h, where each weight set vector, W^h, contains n weights (corresponding to the n hidden layer inputs). For the sake of simplicity, let's assume that we only have one output neuron in our output layer. The weight set vector for this neuron is therefore the following:

$$W^h_1 : w^{h1}_1, w^{h1}_2, \ldots, w^{h1}_n$$

Again, since we are multiplying vectors together, we use the dot product calculation, which will compute the following scalar representing our net input, z:

$$z = \sum_{i=1}^{n} w^{h1}_i h^1_i + bias$$

In `MLlib`'s MLPC, the output neurons use the softmax function as the activation function, which extends logistic regression by predicting k classes instead of a standard binary classification. This function takes the following form:

$$\phi(z) = \sigma(z) = \frac{e^z}{\sum_{k=1}^{K} e^{z_k}}$$

Therefore, the number of nodes in the output layer corresponds to the number of possible classes that you wish to predict from. For example, if your use case has five possible classes, then you would train an MLP with five nodes in the output layer. The final output from the activation function is therefore the prediction that the output neuron in question makes, as illustrated in *Figure 7.4*:

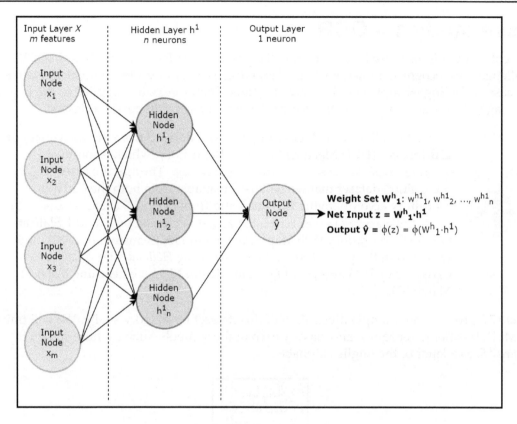

Figure 7.4: Output layer net input and output

Note that *Figure 7.4* illustrates the initial **forward propagation** of the MLP, whereby input data is propagated to the hidden layer and the output from the hidden layer is propagated to the output layer where the final output is computed. `MLlib`'s MLPC thereafter uses **backwards propagation** to train the neural network and learn the model where the difference between the actual output and the desired output is minimized via an iterative weight adjustment process. MLPC achieves this by seeking to minimize a **loss function**. A loss function calculates a measure of the price paid for inaccurate predictions regarding classification problems. The specific loss function that MLPC employs is the **logistic loss function**, where predictions made with a high value of confidence are penalized less. To learn more about loss functions, please visit `https://en.wikipedia.org/wiki/Loss_functions_for_classification`.

Case study 1 – OCR

A great real-world use case to demonstrate the power of MLPs is that of OCR. In OCR, the challenge is to recognize human writing, classifying each handwritten symbol as a letter. In the case of the English alphabet, there are 26 letters. Therefore, when applied to the English language, OCR is actually a classification problem that has $k = 26$ possible classes!

The dataset that we will be using has been derived from the **University of California's** (**UCI**) Machine Learning Repository, which is found at `https://archive.ics.uci.edu/ml/index.php`. The specific letter recognition dataset that we will use, available from both the GitHub repository accompanying this book and from `https://archive.ics.uci.edu/ml/datasets/letter+recognition`, was created by David J. Slate at Odesta Corporation; 1890 Maple Ave; Suite 115; Evanston, IL 60201, and was used in the paper *Letter Recognition Using Holland-style Adaptive Classifiers* by P. W. Frey and D. J. Slate (from Machine Learning Vol 6 #2 March 91).

Figure 7.5 provides an example illustration of this dataset rendered visually. We will train an MLP classifier to recognize and classify each of the symbols, such as those shown in *Figure 7.5*, as a letter of the English alphabet:

Figure 7.5: Letter recognition dataset

Input data

Before we delve further into the schema of our specific dataset, let's first understand how a MLP will actually help us with this problem. Firstly, as we saw in `Chapter 5`, *Unsupervised Learning Using Apache Spark*, when studying image segmentation, images can be broken down into a matrix of either pixel-intensity values (for grayscale images) or pixel RGB values (for images with color). A single vector containing (m x n) numerical elements can then be generated, corresponding to the pixel height (m) and width (n) of the image.

Training architecture

Now, imagine that we want to train an MLP using our entire letter recognition dataset, as illustrated in *Figure 7.6*:

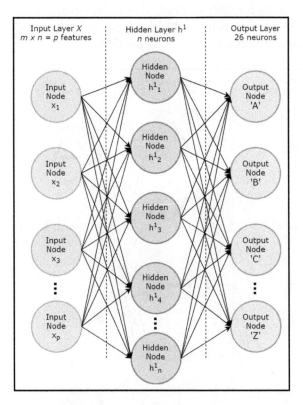

Figure 7.6: Multilayer perceptron for letter recognition

In our MLP, we have p (= m x n) neurons in our input layer that represent the p pixel-intensity values from our image. A single hidden layer has n neurons, and the output layer has 26 neurons that represent the 26 possible classes or letters in the English alphabet. When training this neural network, since we do not know initially what weights should be assigned to each layer, we initialize the weights randomly and perform a first iteration of forward propagation. We then iteratively employ backwards propagation to train the neural network, resulting in a set of weights that have been optimized so that the predictions/classifications made by the output layer are as accurate as possible.

Detecting patterns in the hidden layer

The job of the neurons in the hidden layer is to learn to detect patterns within the input data. In our case, the neurons in the hidden layer(s) will detect the presence of certain substructures that constitute a wider symbol. This is illustrated in *Figure 7.7*, where we assume that the first three neurons in the hidden layer learn to recognize forward slash, back slash and horizontal line type patterns respectively:

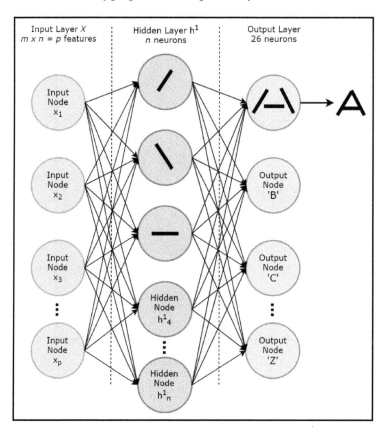

Figure 7.7: Neurons in the hidden layer detect patterns and substructures

Classifying in the output layer

In our neural network, the first neuron in the output layer is trained to decide whether a given symbol is the uppercase English letter *A*. Assuming that the first three neurons in the hidden layer fire, we would expect the first neuron in the output layer to fire and the remaining 25 neurons not to fire. Our MLP would then classify this symbol as the letter *A*!

Note that our training architecture employed only a single hidden layer, which would only be able to learn very simple patterns. By adding more hidden layers, an ANN can learn more complicated patterns at the cost of computational complexity, resources, and training runtime. However, with the advent of distributed storage and processing technologies, as discussed in Chapter 1, *The Big Data Ecosystem*, where huge volumes of data may be stored in memory and a large number of calculations may be processed on that data in a distributed manner, today we are able to train extremely complex neural networks with architecture that may contain large numbers of hidden layers and hidden neurons. Such complex neural networks are currently being applied to a broad range of applications, including facial recognition, speech recognition, real-time threat detection, image-based searching, fraud detection, and advances in healthcare.

MLPs in Apache Spark

Let's return to our dataset and train an MLP in Apache Spark to recognize and classify letters from the English alphabet. If you open ocr-data/letter-recognition.data in any text editor, from either the GitHub repository accompanying this book or from UCI's machine learning repository, you will find 20,000 rows of data, described by the following schema:

Column name	Data type	Description
lettr	String	English letter (one of 26 values, from A to Z)
x-box	Integer	Horizontal position of box
y-box	Integer	Vertical position of box
width	Integer	Width of box
high	Integer	Height of box
onpix	Integer	Total number of on pixels
x-bar	Integer	Mean *x* of on pixels in the box
y-bar	Integer	Mean *y* of on pixels in the box
x2bar	Integer	Mean *x* variance
y2bar	Integer	Mean *y* variance

xybar	Integer	Mean x y correlation
x2ybr	Integer	Mean of $x * x * y$
xy2br	Integer	Mean of $x * y * y$
x-ege	Integer	Mean edge count left to right
xegvy	Integer	Correlation of x-ege with y
y-ege	Integer	Mean edge count, bottom to top
yegvx	Integer	Correlation of y-ege with x

This dataset describes 16 numerical attributes representing statistical features of the pixel distribution based on scanned character images, such as those illustrated in *Figure 7.5*. These attributes have been standardized and scaled linearly to a range of integer values from 0 to 15. For each row, a label column called lettr denotes the letter of the English alphabet that it represents, where no feature vector maps to more than one class—that is, each feature vector maps to only one letter in the English alphabet.

You will have noticed that we are not using the pixel data from the *raw* images themselves, but rather statistical features derived from the distribution of the pixels. However, using what we have learned from Chapter 5, *Unsupervised Learning Using Apache Spark*, when we looked at specifically converting images into numerical feature vectors, the exact same steps that we will look at in a moment may be followed to train an MLP classifier using the raw images themselves.

Let's now use this dataset to train an MLP classifier to recognize symbols and classify them as letters from the English alphabet:

The following subsections describe each of the pertinent cells in the corresponding Jupyter notebook for this use case, called chp07-01-multilayer-perceptron-classifier.ipynb. This notebook can be found in the GitHub repository accompanying this book.

1. First, we import the prerequisite PySpark libraries as normal, including MLlib's MultilayerPerceptronClassifier classifier and MulticlassClassificationEvaluator evaluator respectively, as shown in the following code:

```
import findspark
findspark.init()
from pyspark import SparkContext, SparkConf
from pyspark.sql import SQLContext
from pyspark.ml.feature import VectorAssembler
from pyspark.ml.classification import
```

```
MultilayerPerceptronClassifier
from pyspark.ml.evaluation import MulticlassClassificationEvaluator
```

2. After instantiating a Spark context, we are now ready to ingest our dataset into a Spark dataframe. Note that in our case, we have preprocessed the dataset into CSV format, where we have converted the `lettr` column from a `string` datatype to a `numeric` datatype representing one of the 26 characters in the English alphabet. This preprocessed CSV file is available in the GitHub repository accompanying this book. Once we have ingested this CSV file into a Spark dataframe, we then generate feature vectors using `VectorAssembler`, comprising the 16 feature columns, as usual. The resulting Spark dataframe, called `vectorised_df`, therefore contains two columns—the numeric `label` column, representing one of the 26 characters in the English alphabet, and the `features` column, containing our feature vectors:

```
letter_recognition_df = sqlContext.read
    .format('com.databricks.spark.csv')
    .options(header = 'true', inferschema = 'true')
    .load('letter-recognition.csv')
feature_columns = ['x-box','y-box','width','high','onpix','x-bar',
    'y-bar','x2bar','y2bar','xybar','x2ybr','xy2br','x-ege','xegvy',
    'y-ege','yegvx']
vector_assembler = VectorAssembler(inputCols = feature_columns,
    outputCol = 'features')
vectorised_df = vector_assembler.transform(letter_recognition_df)
    .withColumnRenamed('lettr', 'label').select('label', 'features')
```

3. Next, we split our dataset into training and test datasets with a ratio of 75% to 25% respectively, using the following code:

```
train_df, test_df = vectorised_df
    .randomSplit([0.75, 0.25], seed=12345)
```

4. We are now ready to train our MLP classifier. First, we must define the size of the respective layers of our neural network. We do this by defining a Python list with the following elements:

   - The first element defines the size of the input layer. In our case, we have 16 features in our dataset, and so we set this element to `16`.
   - The next elements define the sizes of the intermediate hidden layers. We shall define two hidden layers of sizes `8` and `4` respectively.

- The final element defines the size of the output layer. In our case, we have 26 possible classes representing the 26 letters of the English alphabet, and so we set this element to 26:

```
layers = [16, 8, 4, 26]
```

5. Now that we have defined the architecture of our neural network, we can train an MLP using MLlib's MultilayerPerceptronClassifier classifier and fit it to the training dataset, as shown in the following code. Remember that MLlib's MultilayerPerceptronClassifier classifier uses the sigmoid activation function for hidden neurons and the softmax activation function for output neurons:

```
multilayer_perceptron_classifier = MultilayerPerceptronClassifier(
    maxIter = 100, layers = layers, blockSize = 128, seed = 1234)
multilayer_perceptron_classifier_model =
    multilayer_perceptron_classifier.fit(train_df)
```

6. We can now apply our trained MLP classifier to the test dataset in order to predict which of the 26 letters of the English alphabet the 16 numerical pixel-related features represent, as follows:

```
test_predictions_df = multilayer_perceptron_classifier_model
    .transform(test_df)
print("TEST DATASET PREDICTIONS AGAINST ACTUAL LABEL: ")
test_predictions_df.select("label", "features", "probability",
    "prediction").show()
```

```
TEST DATASET PREDICTIONS AGAINST ACTUAL LABEL:
+-----+-------------------+--------------------+----------+
|label| features| probability|prediction|
+-----+-------------------+--------------------+----------+
|    0|[1.0,0.0,2.0,0.0,...|[0.62605849526384...|       0.0|
|    0|[1.0,0.0,2.0,0.0,...|[0.62875656935176...|       0.0|
|    0|[1.0,0.0,2.0,0.0,...|[0.62875656935176...|       0.0|
+-----+-------------------+--------------------+----------+
```

7. Next, we compute the accuracy of our trained MLP classifier on the test dataset using the following code. In our case, it performs very poorly, with an accuracy rate of only 34%. We can conclude from this that an MLP with two hidden layers of sizes 8 and 4 respectively performs very poorly in recognizing and classifying letters from scanned images in the case of our dataset:

```
prediction_and_labels = test_predictions_df
    .select("prediction", "label")
accuracy_evaluator = MulticlassClassificationEvaluator(
```

```
    metricName = "accuracy")
precision_evaluator = MulticlassClassificationEvaluator(
    metricName = "weightedPrecision")
recall_evaluator = MulticlassClassificationEvaluator(
    metricName = "weightedRecall")
print("Accuracy on Test Dataset = %g" % accuracy_evaluator
    .evaluate(prediction_and_labels))
print("Precision on Test Dataset = %g" % precision_evaluator
    .evaluate(prediction_and_labels))
print("Recall on Test Dataset = %g" % recall_evaluator
    .evaluate(prediction_and_labels))

Accuracy on Test Dataset = 0.339641
Precision on Test Dataset = 0.313333
Recall on Test Dataset = 0.339641
```

8. How can we increase the accuracy of our neural classifier? To answer this question, we must revisit our definition of what the hidden layers do. Remember that the job of the neurons in the hidden layers is to learn to detect patterns within the input data. Therefore, defining more hidden neurons in our neural architecture should increase the ability of our neural network to detect more patterns at greater resolutions. To test this hypothesis, we shall increase the number of neurons in our two hidden layers to 16 and 12 respectively, as shown in the following code. Then, we retrain our MLP classifier and reapply it to the test dataset. This results in a far better performing model, with an accuracy rate of 72%:

```
new_layers = [16, 16, 12, 26]
new_multilayer_perceptron_classifier =
    MultilayerPerceptronClassifier(maxIter = 400,
        layers = new_layers, blockSize = 128, seed = 1234)
new_multilayer_perceptron_classifier_model =
    new_multilayer_perceptron_classifier.fit(train_df)
new_test_predictions_df =
    new_multilayer_perceptron_classifier_model.transform(test_df)
print("New Accuracy on Test Dataset = %g" % accuracy_evaluator
    .evaluate(new_test_predictions_df
    .select("prediction", "label")))
```

Convolutional neural networks

We have seen how MLPs, which receive a single input vector that is then transformed through one or more intermediate hidden layers, can be used to recognize and classify small images such as letters and digits in OCR. However, one limitation of MLPs is their ability to scale with larger images, taking into account not just individual pixel intensity or RGB values, but the height, width, and depth of the image itself.

Convolutional neural networks (**CNNs**) assume that the input data is of a grid-like topology, and so they are predominantly used to recognize and classify objects in images since an image can be represented as a grid of pixels.

End-to-end neural architecture

The end-to-end architecture of a convolutional neural network is illustrated in *Figure 7.8*:

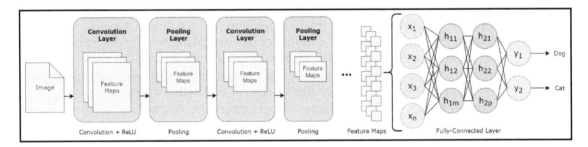

Figure 7.8: Convolutional neural network architecture

In the following subsections, we will describe each of the layers and transformations that constitute a CNN.

Input layer

Given that CNNs are predominantly used to classify images, the input data into CNNs consists of image matrices of the dimensions h (height in pixels), w (width in pixels) and d (depth). In the case of RGB images, the depth would be three corresponding, to the three color channels, **red**, **green**, and **blue** (**RGB**). This is illustrated in *Figure 7.9*:

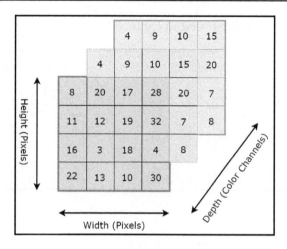

Figure 7.9: Image matrix dimensions

Convolution layers

The next transformations that occur in the CNN are processed in *convolution* layers. The purpose of the convolution layers is to detect features in the image, which is achieved through the use of **filters** (also called kernels). Imagine taking a magnifying glass and looking at an image, starting at the top-left of the image. As we move the magnifying glass from left to right and top to bottom, we detect the different features in each of the locations that our magnifying glass moves over. At a high level, this is the job of the convolution layers, where the magnifying glass represents the filter or kernel and the size of each step that the filter takes, normally pixel by pixel, is referred to as the **stride** size. The output of a convolution layer is called a **feature map**.

Let's look at an example to understand the processes undertaken within a convolution layer better. Imagine that we have an image that is 3 pixels (height) by 3 pixels (width). For the sake of simplicity, we will overlook the third dimension representing the image depth in our example, but note that real-world convolutions are computed in three dimensions for RGB images. Next, imagine that our filter is a matrix of 2 pixels (height) by 2 pixels (width) and that our stride size is 1 pixel.

These respective matrices are illustrated in *Figure 7.10*:

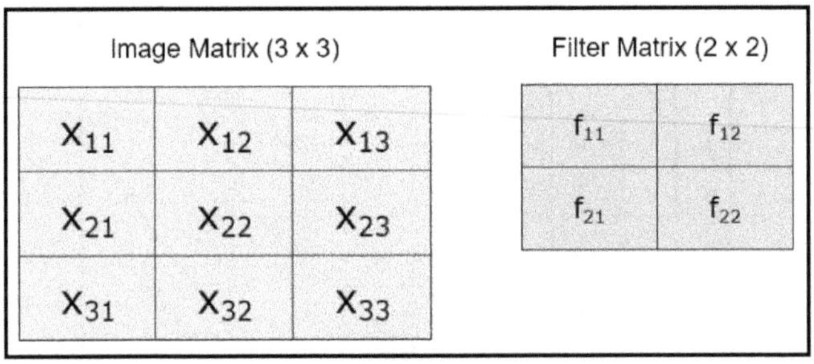

Image Matrix (3 x 3)			Filter Matrix (2 x 2)	
X_{11}	X_{12}	X_{13}	f_{11}	f_{12}
X_{21}	X_{22}	X_{23}	f_{21}	f_{22}
X_{31}	X_{32}	X_{33}		

Figure 7.10: Image matrix and filter matrix

First, we place our filter matrix at the top-left corner of our image matrix and perform a **matrix multiplication** of the two at that location. We then move the filter matrix to the right by our stride size—1 pixel—and perform a matrix multiplication at that location. We continue this process until the filter matrix has traversed the entire image matrix. The resulting feature map matrix is illustrated in *Figure 7.11*:

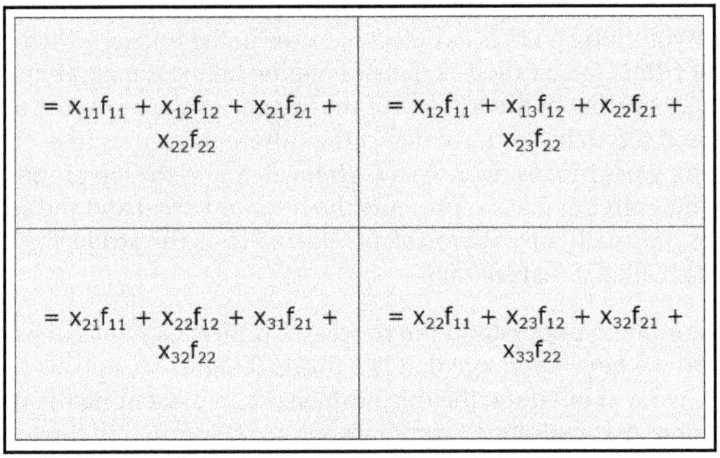

$= X_{11}f_{11} + X_{12}f_{12} + X_{21}f_{21} + X_{22}f_{22}$	$= X_{12}f_{11} + X_{13}f_{12} + X_{22}f_{21} + X_{23}f_{22}$
$= X_{21}f_{11} + X_{22}f_{12} + X_{31}f_{21} + X_{32}f_{22}$	$= X_{22}f_{11} + X_{23}f_{12} + X_{32}f_{21} + X_{33}f_{22}$

Figure 7.11: Feature map

Note that the feature map is smaller in its dimensions than the input matrix of the convolution layer. To ensure that the dimensions of the output match the dimensions of the input, a layer of zero-value pixels is added in a process called **padding**. Also note that the filter must have the same number of channels as the input image—so in the case of RGB images, the filter must also have three channels.

So, how do convolutions help a neural network to learn? To answer this question, we must revisit the concept of filters. Filters themselves are matrices of *weights* that are trained to detect specific patterns within an image, and different filters can be used to detect different patterns, such as edges and other features. For example, if we use a filter that has been pretrained to detect simple edges, as we pass this filter over an image, the convolution computation will output a high-valued real number (as a result of matrix multiplication and summation) if an edge is present and a low-valued real number if an edge is not present.

As the filter finishes traversing the entire image, the output is a feature map matrix that represents the convolutions of this filter over all parts of the image. By using different filters during different convolutions per layer, we get different feature maps, which form the output of the convolution layer.

Rectified linear units

As with other neural networks, an activation function defines the output of a node and is used so that our neural network can learn nonlinear functions. Note that our input data (the RGB pixels making up the images) is itself nonlinear, so we need a nonlinear activation function. **Rectified linear units (ReLUs)** are commonly used in CNNs, and are defined as follows:

$$\phi(z) = R(z) = max(0, z)$$

In other words, the ReLU function returns 0 for every negative value in its input data, and returns the value itself for every positive value in its input data. This is shown in *Figure 7.12*:

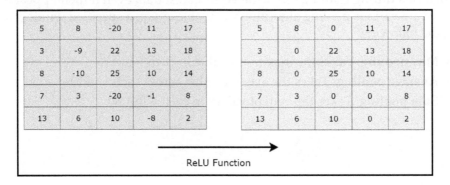

Figure 7.12: ReLU function

The ReLU function can be plotted as shown in *Figure 7.13*:

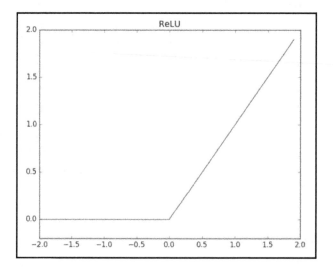

Figure 7.13: ReLU function graph

Pooling layers

The next transformations that occur in the CNN are processed in *pooling* layers. The goal of the pooling layers is to reduce the dimensionality of the feature maps output by the convolution layers (but not their depth) while preserving the spatial variance of the original input data. In other words, the size of the data is reduced in order to reduce computational complexity, memory requirements, and training times while overcoming over fitting so that patterns detected during training can be detected in test data even if their appearance varies. There are various pooling algorithms available, given a specified window size, including the following:

- **Max pooling**: Takes the maximum value in each window
- **Average pooling**: Takes the average value across each window
- **Sum pooling**: Takes the sum of values in each window

Figure 7.14 shows the effect of performing max pooling on a 4 x 4 feature map using a 2 x 2 window size:

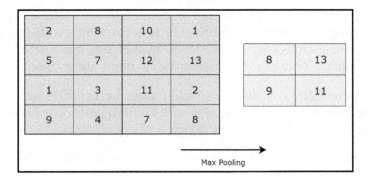

Figure 7.14: Max pooling on a 4 x 4 feature map using a 2 x 2 window

Fully connected layer

After the 3-D input data has been transformed through a series of convolution and pooling layers, a fully connected layer flattens the feature maps output by the last convolution and pooling layer into a long 1-D feature vector, which is then used as the input data for a regular ANN in which all of the neurons in each layer are connected to all of the neurons in the previous layer.

Output layer

The output neurons in this ANN then use an activation function such as the softmax function (as seen in the MLP classifier) to classify the outputs and thereby recognize and classify the objects contained in the input image data!

Case study 2 – image recognition

In this case study, we will use a pretrained CNN to recognize and classify objects in images that it has never encountered before.

InceptionV3 via TensorFlow

The pretrained CNN that we will use is called **Inception-v3**. This deep CNN has been trained on the **ImageNet** image database (an academic benchmark for computer vision algorithms containing a vast library of labelled images covering a wide range of nouns) and can classify entire images into 1,000 classes found in everyday life, such as "pizza", "plastic bag", "red wine", "desk", "orange", and "basketball", to name just a few.

The Inception-v3 deep CNN was developed and trained by **TensorFlow** ™, an open source machine learning framework and software library for high-performance numerical computation originally developed within Google's AI organization.

To learn more about TensorFlow, Inception-v3, and ImageNet, please visit the following links:

- **ImageNet:** http://www.image-net.org/
- **TensorFlow:** https://www.tensorflow.org/
- **Inception-v3:** https://www.tensorflow.org/tutorials/images/image_recognition

Deep learning pipelines for Apache Spark

In this case study, we will access the Inception-v3 TensorFlow deep CNN via a third-party Spark package called `sparkdl`. This Spark package has been developed by Databricks, a company formed by the original creators of Apache Spark, and provides high-level APIs for scalable deep learning within Apache Spark.

To learn more about Databricks and `sparkdl`, please visit the following links:

- **Databricks**: https://databricks.com/
- **sparkdl**: https://github.com/databricks/spark-deep-learning

Image library

The images that we will use to test the pretrained Inception-v3 deep CNN have been selected from the **Open Images v4** dataset, a collection of over 9 million images that have been released under the Creative Common Attribution license, and which may be found at https://storage.googleapis.com/openimages/web/index.html.

In the GitHub repository accompanying this book, you can find 30 images of birds (image-recognition-data/birds) and 30 images of planes (image-recognition-data/planes) respectively. *Figure 7.15* shows a couple of examples of the images that you might find in these test datasets:

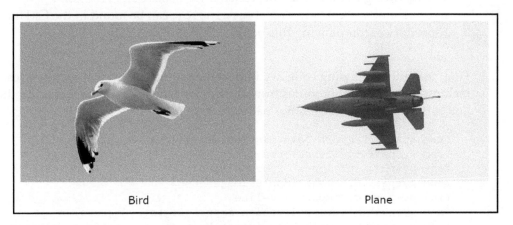

Figure 7.15: Example images from the Open Images v4 dataset

Our goal in this case study will be to apply the pretrained Inception-v3 deep CNN to these test images and quantify the accuracy of a trained classifier model when it comes to distinguishing between images of birds and planes within a single test dataset.

PySpark image recognition application

Note that for the purposes of this case study, we will not be using Jupyter notebooks for development but rather standard Python code files with the .py file extension. This case study provides a first glimpse into how a production-grade pipeline should be developed and executed; rather than instantiating a SparkContext explicitly within our code, we will instead submit our code and all its dependencies to spark-submit (including any third-party Spark packages, such as sparkdl) via the Linux command line.

Let's now take a look at how we can use the Inception-v3 deep CNN via PySpark to classify test images. In our Python-based image-recognition application, we perform the following steps (numbered to correspond to the numbered comments in our Python code file):

The following Python code file, called `chp07-02-convolutional-neural-network-transfer-learning.py`, can be found in the GitHub repository accompanying this book.

1. First, using the following code, we import the required Python dependencies, including the relevant modules from the third-party `sparkdl` package and the `LogisticRegression` classifier native to `MLlib`:

```
from sparkdl import DeepImageFeaturizer
from pyspark.sql.functions import *
from pyspark.sql import SparkSession
from pyspark.ml.image import ImageSchema
from pyspark.ml import Pipeline
from pyspark.ml.classification import LogisticRegression
from pyspark.ml.evaluation import MulticlassClassificationEvaluator
```

2. Unlike our Jupyter notebook case studies, there is no need to instantiate a `SparkContext`, as this will be done for us when we execute our PySpark application via `spark-submit` on the command line. In this case study, we will create a `SparkSession`, as shown in the following code, that acts as an entry point into the Spark execution environment (even if it is already running) that subsumes SQLContext. We can therefore use `SparkSession` to undertake the same SQL-like operations over data that we have seen previously while still using the Spark Dataset/DataFrame API:

```
spark = SparkSession.builder.appName("Convolutional Neural Networks
- Transfer Learning - Image Recognition").getOrCreate()
```

3. As of Version 2.3, Spark provides native support for image data sources via its `MLlib` API. In this step, we invoke the `readImages` method on `MLlib`'s `ImageSchema` class to load our bird and plane test images from the local filesystem into Spark dataframes called `birds_df` and `planes_df` respectively. We then label all images of birds with the 0 literal and label all images of planes with the 1 literal, as follows:

```
path_to_img_directory = 'chapter07/data/image-recognition-data'
birds_df = ImageSchema.readImages(path_to_img_directory + "/birds")
    .withColumn("label", lit(0))
```

```
planes_df = ImageSchema.readImages(path_to_img_directory +
    "/planes").withColumn("label", lit(1))
```

4. Now that we have loaded our test images into separate Spark dataframes differentiated by their label, we consolidate them into single training and test dataframes accordingly. We achieve this by using the `unionAll` method via the Spark dataframe API, which simply appends one dataframe onto another, as shown in the following code:

```
planes_train_df, planes_test_df = planes_df
    .randomSplit([0.75, 0.25], seed=12345)
birds_train_df, birds_test_df = birds_df
    .randomSplit([0.75, 0.25], seed=12345)
train_df = planes_train_df.unionAll(birds_train_df)
test_df = planes_test_df.unionAll(birds_test_df)
```

5. As with previous case studies, we need to generate feature vectors from our input data. However, rather than training a deep CNN from scratch—which could take many days, even with distributed technologies—we will take advantage of the pretrained Inception-v3 deep CNN. To do this, we will use a process called **transfer learning**. In this process, knowledge gained while solving one machine learning problem is applied to a different but related problem. To use transfer learning in our case study, we employ the `DeepImageFeaturizer` module of the third-party `sparkdl` Spark package. The `DeepImageFeaturizer` not only transforms our images into numeric features, it also performs fast transfer learning by peeling off the last layer of a pretrained neural network and then uses the output from all the previous layers as features for a standard classification algorithm. In our case, the `DeepImageFeaturizer` will be peeling off the last layer of the pretrained Inception-v3 deep CNN, as follows:

```
featurizer = DeepImageFeaturizer(inputCol = "image",
    outputCol = "features", modelName = "InceptionV3")
```

6. Now that we have the features from all previous layers of the pretrained Inception-v3 deep CNN extracted via transfer learning, we input them into a classification algorithm. In our case, we will use `MLlib`'s `LogisticRegression` classifier, as follows:

```
logistic_regression = LogisticRegression(maxIter = 20,
    regParam = 0.05, elasticNetParam = 0.3, labelCol = "label")
```

7. To execute the transfer learning and logistic regression model training, we build a standard `pipeline` and `fit` that pipeline to our training dataframe, as follows:

```
pipeline = Pipeline(stages = [featurizer, logistic_regression])
model = pipeline.fit(train_df)
```

8. Now that we have a trained classification model, using the features derived by the Inception-v3 deep CNN, we apply our trained logistic regression model to our test dataframe to make predictions as normal, as shown in the following code:

```
test_predictions_df = model.transform(test_df)
test_predictions_df.select("image.origin", "prediction")
    .show(truncate=False)
```

9. Finally, we quantify the accuracy of our model on the test dataframe using MLlib's `MulticlassClassificationEvaluator`, as follows:

```
accuracy_evaluator = MulticlassClassificationEvaluator(
    metricName = "accuracy")
print("Accuracy on Test Dataset = %g" % accuracy_evaluator
    .evaluate(test_predictions_df.select("label", "prediction")))
```

Spark submit

We are now ready to run our image recognition application! Since it is a Spark application, we can execute it via `spark-submit` on the Linux command line. To do this, navigate to the directory where we installed Apache Spark (see Chapter 2, *Setting Up a Local Development Environment*). Then, we can execute the `spark-submit` program by passing it the following command-line arguments:

- `--master`: The Spark Master URL.
- `--packages`: The third-party libraries and dependencies required for the Spark application to work. In our case, our image-recognition application is dependent on the availability of the `sparkdl` third-party library.

- `--py-files`: Since our image-recognition application is a PySpark application, we pass the filesystem paths to any Python code files that our application is dependent on. In our case, since our image-recognition application is self-contained within a single code file, there are no further dependencies to pass to `spark-submit`.
- The final argument is the path to the Python code file containing our Spark driver program, namely `chp07-02-convolutional-neural-network-transfer-learning.py`.

The final commands to execute, therefore, look as follows:

```
> cd {SPARK_HOME}
> bin/spark-submit --master spark://192.168.56.10:7077 --packages
databricks:spark-deep-learning:1.2.0-spark2.3-s_2.11 chapter07/chp07-02-
convolutional-neural-network-transfer-learning.py
```

Image-recognition results

Assuming that the image-recognition application ran successfully, you should see the following results output to the console:

Origin	Prediction
planes/plane-005.jpg	1.0
planes/plane-008.jpg	1.0
planes/plane-009.jpg	1.0
planes/plane-016.jpg	1.0
planes/plane-017.jpg	0.0
planes/plane-018.jpg	1.0
birds/bird-005.jpg	0.0
birds/bird-008.jpg	0.0
birds/bird-009.jpg	0.0
birds/bird-016.jpg	0.0
birds/bird-017.jpg	0.0
birds/bird-018.jpg	0.0

The Origin column refers to the absolute filesystem path of the image, and the value in the Prediction column is 1.0 if our model predicts that the object in the image is a plane and 0.0 if our model predicts that the object in the image is a bird. Our model has an astonishingly high accuracy of 92% when run on the test dataset. The only mistake that our model made was on plane-017.jpg, illustrated in *Figure 7.16*, which was incorrectly classified as a bird when it was in fact a plane:

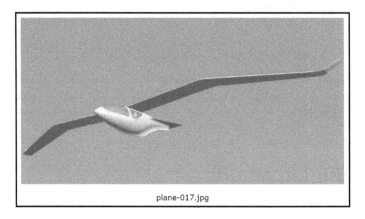

plane-017.jpg

Figure 7.16: Incorrect classification of plane-017.jpg

If we look at plane-017.jpg in *Figure 7.16*, we can quickly understand why the model made this mistake. Though it is a man-made plane, it has been physically modeled to look like a bird for increased efficiency and aerodynamic purposes.

In this case study, we used a pretrained CNN to featurize images. We then passed the resulting features to a standard logistic regression algorithm to predict whether a given image is a bird or a plane.

Case study 3 – image prediction

In case study 2 (image recognition), we still explicitly labelled our test images before training our final logistic regression classifier. In this case study, we will simply send random images to the pretrained Inception-v3 deep CNN without labeling them and let the CNN itself classify the objects contained within the images. Again, we will take advantage of the third-party sparkdl Spark package to access the pretrained Inception-v3 CNN.

The assortment of random images that we will use have again been downloaded from the **Open Images v4 dataset**, and may be found in the GitHub repository accompanying this book under `image-recognition-data/assorted`. *Figure 7.17* shows a couple of typical images that you may find in this test dataset:

snowman.jpg   fork.jpg

Figure 7.17: Assortment of random images

PySpark image-prediction application

In our Python-based image-prediction application, we go through the following steps (numbered to correspond to the numbered comments in our Python code file):

> The following Python code file, called `chp07-03-convolutional-neural-network-image-predictor.py`, can be found in the GitHub repository accompanying this book.

1. First, we import the required Python dependencies as usual, including the `DeepImagePredictor` class from the third-party `sparkdl` Spark package, as shown in the following code:

```
from sparkdl import DeepImagePredictor
from pyspark.sql import SparkSession
from pyspark.ml.image import ImageSchema
```

2. Next, we create a `SparkSession` that acts as an entry point into the Spark execution environment, as follows:

```
spark = SparkSession.builder.appName("Convolutional Neural Networks
  - Deep Image Predictor").getOrCreate()
```

3. We then load our assortment of random images into a Spark dataframe using the `readImages` method of the `ImageSchema` class that we first encountered in the previous case study, as shown in the following code:

```
assorted_images_df = ImageSchema.readImages(
    "chapter07/data/image-recognition-data/assorted")
```

4. Finally, we pass our Spark dataframe containing our assortment of random images to `sparkdl`'s `DeepImagePredictor`, which will apply a specified pretrained neural network to the images in an effort to classify the objects found within them. In our case, we will be using the pretrained Inception-v3 deep CNN. We also tell the `DeepImagePredictor` to return the top 10 (`topK=10`) predicted classifications for each image in descending order of confidence, as follows:

```
deep_image_predictor = DeepImagePredictor(inputCol = "image",
    outputCol = "predicted_label", modelName = "InceptionV3",
    decodePredictions = True, topK = 10)
predictions_df = deep_image_predictor.transform(assorted_images_df)
predictions_df.select("image.origin", "predicted_label")
    .show(truncate = False)
```

To run this PySpark image-prediction application, we again invoke `spark-submit` via the command line, as follows:

```
> cd {SPARK_HOME}
> bin/spark-submit --master spark://192.168.56.10:7077 --packages
databricks:spark-deep-learning:1.2.0-spark2.3-s_2.11 chapter07/chp07-03-
convolutional-neural-network-image-predictor.py
```

Image-prediction results

Assuming that the image-prediction application ran successfully, you should see the following results output to the console:

Origin	First Predicted Label
`assorted/snowman.jpg`	Teddy
`assorted/bicycle.jpg`	Mountain Bike
`assorted/house.jpg`	Library
`assorted/bus.jpg`	Trolley Bus
`assorted/banana.jpg`	Banana
`assorted/pizza.jpg`	Pizza
`assorted/toilet.jpg`	Toilet Seat
`assorted/knife.jpg`	Cleaver
`assorted/apple.jpg`	Granny Smith (Apple)
`assorted/pen.jpg`	Ballpoint
`assorted/lion.jpg`	Lion
`assorted/saxophone.jpg`	Saxophone
`assorted/zebra.jpg`	Zebra
`assorted/fork.jpg`	Spatula
`assorted/car.jpg`	Convertible

As you can see, the pretrained Inception-v3 deep CNN has an astonishing ability to recognize and classify the objects found in images. Though the images provided in this case study were relatively simple, the Inception-v3 CNN has a top-five error rate— how often the model fails to predict the correct answer as one of its top five guesses—of just 3.46% on the ImageNet image database. Remember that the Inception-v3 CNN attempts to classify entire images into 1,000 classes, hence a top-5 error rate of just 3.46% is truly impressive, and clearly demonstrates the learning ability and power of not only convolution neural networks but ANNs in general when detecting and learning patterns!

Summary

In this chapter, we went on a hands-on exploration through the exciting and cutting-edge world of deep learning. We developed applications to recognize and classify objects in images with astonishingly high rates of accuracy, and demonstrated the truly impressive learning ability of ANNs to detect and learn patterns in input data.

In the next chapter, we will extend our deployment of machine learning models beyond batch processing in order to learn from data and make predictions in real time!

Real-Time Machine Learning Using Apache Spark

8

In this chapter, we will extend our deployment of machine learning models beyond batch processing in order to learn from data, make predictions, and identify trends in real time! We will develop and deploy a real-time stream processing and machine learning application comprised of the following high-level technologies:

- Apache Kafka producer application
- Apache Kafka consumer application
- Apache Spark's Structured Streaming engine
- Apache Spark's machine learning library, `MLlib`

Distributed streaming platform

So far in this book, we have been performing batch processing—that is, we have been provided with bounded raw data files and processed that data as a group. As we saw in Chapter 1, *The Big Data Ecosystem*, stream processing differs from batch processing in the fact that data is processed as and when individual units, or streams, of data arrive. We also saw in Chapter 1, *The Big Data Ecosystem*, how **Apache Kafka**, as a distributed *streaming platform*, allows us to move real-time data between systems and applications in a fault-tolerant and reliable manner via a logical streaming architecture comprising of the following components:

- **Producers**: Applications that generate and send messages
- **Consumers**: Applications that subscribe to and consume messages

- **Topics**: Streams of records belonging to a particular category and stored as a sequence of ordered and immutable records partitioned and replicated across a distributed cluster
- **Stream processors**: Applications that process messages in a certain manner, such as data transformations and machine learning models

A simplified illustration of this logical streaming architecture is shown in *Figure 8.1*:

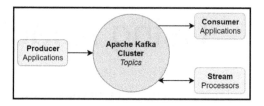

Figure 8.1: Apache Kafka logical streaming architecture

Distributed stream processing engines

Apache Kafka allows us to *move* real-time data reliably between systems and applications. But we still need some sort of processing engine to process and transform that real-time data in order ultimately to derive value from it based on the use case in question. Fortunately, there are a number of *stream processing engines* available to allow us to do this, including—but not limited—to the following:

- **Apache Spark:** https://spark.apache.org/
- **Apache Storm:** http://storm.apache.org/
- **Apache Flink:** https://flink.apache.org/
- **Apache Samza:** http://samza.apache.org/
- **Apache Kafka (via its Streams API):** https://kafka.apache.org/documentation/
- **KSQL:** https://www.confluent.io/product/ksql/

Though a detailed comparison of the available stream processing engines is beyond the scope of this book, you are encouraged to explore the preceding links and study the differing architectures available. For the purposes of this chapter, we will be using Apache Spark's Structured Streaming engine as our stream processing engine of choice.

Streaming using Apache Spark

At the time of writing, there are two stream processing APIs available in Spark:

- **Spark Streaming (DStreams):** `https://spark.apache.org/docs/latest/streaming-programming-guide.html`
- **Structured Streaming:** `https://spark.apache.org/docs/latest/structured-streaming-programming-guide.html`

Spark Streaming (DStreams)

Spark Streaming (DStreams) extends the core Spark API and works by dividing real-time data streams into *input batches* that are then processed by Spark's core API, resulting in a final stream of *processed batches*, as illustrated in *Figure 8.2*. A sequence of RDDs form what is known as a *discretized stream* (or DStream), which represents the continuous stream of data:

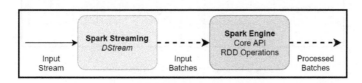

Figure 8.2: Spark Streaming (DStreams)

Structured Streaming

Structured Streaming, on the other hand, is a newer and highly optimized stream processing engine built on the Spark SQL engine in which streaming data can be stored and processed using Spark's Dataset/DataFrame API (see `Chapter 1`, *The Big Data Ecosystem*). As of Spark 2.3, Structured Streaming offers the ability to process data streams using both micro-batch processing, with latencies as low as 100 milliseconds, and *continuous processing*, with latencies as low as 1 millisecond (thereby providing *true* real-time processing). Structured Streaming works by modelling data streams as an unbounded table that is being continuously appended. When a transformation or other type of query is processed on this unbounded table, a results table will be generated that is representative of that moment in time.

After a configurable trigger interval, new data in the data stream is modeled as new rows appended to this unbounded table and the results table is subsequently updated, as illustrated in *Figure 8.3*:

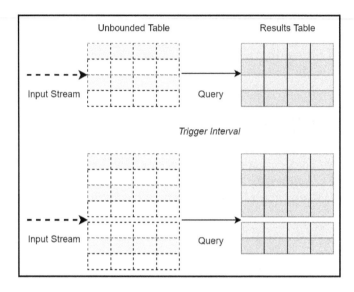

Figure 8.3: Spark Structured Streaming logical model

As streaming data is exposed via the Dataset/DataFrame API, both SQL-like operations (including aggregations and joins) and RDD operations (including map and filtering) can easily be executed on real-time streams of data. Furthermore, Structured Streaming offers features that are designed to cater for data that arrives late, the management and monitoring of streaming queries, and the ability to recover from failures. As such, Structured Streaming is an extremely versatile, efficient, and reliable way to process streaming data with extremely low latencies, and is the stream processing engine that we will use for the remainder of this chapter.

In general, it is advised that developers use this newer and highly optimized engine over Spark Streaming (DStreams). However, since it is a newer API, there may be certain features that are not yet available as of Spark 2.3.2, which will mean the continued occasional usage of the DStreams RDD-based approach while the newer API is being developed.

Stream processing pipeline

In this section, we will develop an end-to-end stream processing pipeline that is capable of streaming data from a source system that generates continuous data, and thereafter able to publish those streams to an Apache Kafka distributed cluster. Our stream processing pipeline will then use Apache Spark to both consume data from Apache Kafka, using its Structured Streaming engine, and apply trained machine learning models to these streams in order to derive insights in real time using MLlib. The end-to-end stream processing pipeline that we will develop is illustrated in *Figure 8.4*:

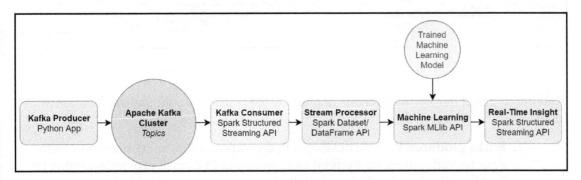

Figure 8.4: Our end-to-end stream processing pipeline

Case study – real-time sentiment analysis

In the case study for this chapter, we will extend the sentiment analysis model that we developed in Chapter 6, *Natural Language Processing Using Apache Spark*, to operate in real time. In Chapter 6, *Natural Language Processing Using Apache Spark*, we trained a decision tree classifier to predict and classify the underlying sentiment of tweets based on a training dataset of historic tweets about airlines. In this chapter, we will apply this trained decision tree classifier to real-time tweets in order to predict their sentiment and identify negative tweets so that airlines may act on them as soon as possible.

Our end-to-end stream processing pipeline can therefore be extended, as illustrated in *Figure 8.5*:

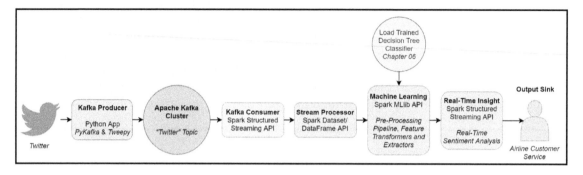

Figure 8.5: Our end-to-end stream processing pipeline for real-time sentiment analysis

The core stages of our stream processing pipeline for real-time sentiment analysis are as follows:

1. **Kafka producer:** We will develop a Python application, using the `pykafka` (an Apache Kafka client for Python) and `tweepy` (a Python library for accessing the Twitter API) libraries that we installed in `Chapter 2`, *Setting Up a Local Development Environment*, to capture tweets about airlines that are being tweeted in real time and to then publish those tweets to an Apache Kafka topic called `twitter`.

2. **Kafka consumer:** We will then develop a Spark application, using its Structured Streaming API, to subscribe to and then consume tweets from the `twitter` topic into a Spark dataframe.

3. **Stream processor and** `MLlib`**:** We will then preprocess the raw textual content of the tweets stored in this Spark dataframe using the same pipeline of feature transformers and feature extractors that we studied and developed in `Chapter 6`, *Natural Language Processing Using Apache Spark*, namely tokenization, removing stop words, stemming, and normalization—before applying the HashingTF transformer to generate feature vectors in real time.

4. **Trained decision tree classifier:** Next, we will load the decision tree classifier that we trained in `Chapter 6`, *Natural Language Processing Using Apache Spark,* and persisted to the local filesystem of our single development node. Once loaded, we will apply this trained decision tree classifier to the Spark dataframe containing our preprocessed feature vectors derived from real time tweets in order to predict and classify their underlying sentiment.

5. **Output sink:** Finally, we will output the results of our sentiment analysis model applied to real-time tweets to a target destination, called an output *sink*. In our case, the output sink will be the *console* sink, one of the built-in output sinks provided natively by the Structured Streaming API. By using this sink, the output is printed to the console/**standard output** (**stdout**) every time there is a trigger. From this console, we will be able to read both the raw textual content of the original tweets and the predicted sentiment classification from our model, namely negative or non-negative. To learn more about the various output sinks available, please visit https://spark.apache.org/docs/latest/structured-streaming-programming-guide.html#output-sinks.

The following subsections describe the technical steps that we will follow to develop, deploy, and run our end-to-end stream processing pipeline for real-time sentiment analysis.

 Note that for the purposes of this case study, we will not be using Jupyter notebooks for development. This is because separate code files are required for the separate components, as described previously. This case study therefore provides another glimpse into how a production-grade pipeline should be developed and executed. Rather than instantiating a SparkContext explicitly within a notebook, we will instead submit our Python code files and all dependencies to spark-submit via the Linux command line.

Start Zookeeper and Kafka Servers

The first step is to ensure that our single-node Kafka cluster is up and running. As described in Chapter 2, *Setting Up a Local Development Environment*, please execute the following commands to start Apache Kafka:

```
> cd {KAFKA_HOME}
> bin/zookeeper-server-start.sh -daemon config/zookeeper.properties
> bin/kafka-server-start.sh -daemon config/server.properties
```

Kafka topic

Next, we need to create a Kafka topic to which our Python Kafka producer application (which we will develop later on) will publish real-time tweets about airlines. In our case, we will call the topic twitter. As demonstrated in Chapter 2, *Setting Up a Local Development Environment*, this can be achieved as follows:

```
> bin/kafka-topics.sh --create --zookeeper 192.168.56.10:2181 --
replication-factor 1 --partitions 1 --topic twitter
```

Twitter developer account

In order for our Python Kafka producer application to capture tweets in real time, we require access to the Twitter API. As of July 2018, a Twitter *developer account*, in addition to a normal Twitter account, must be created and approved in order to access its API. In order to apply for a developer account, please go to `https://apps.twitter.com/`, click on the **Apply for a Developer Account** button, and fill in the required details.

Twitter apps and the Twitter API

Once you have created your Twitter developer account, in order to use the Twitter API, a Twitter *app* must be created. A Twitter app provides authenticated and authorized access to the Twitter API based on the specific purpose of the app that you intend to create. In order to create a Twitter app for the purposes of our real-time sentiment analysis model, please go through the following instructions (valid at the time of writing):

1. Navigate to `https://developer.twitter.com/en/apps`.
2. Select the **Create an App** button.
3. Provide the following mandatory app details:

   ```
   - App Name (max 32 characters) e.g. "Airline Sentiment Analysis"
   - Application Description (max 200 characters) e.g. "This App will
   collect tweets about airlines and apply our previously trained
   decision tree classifier to predict and classify the underlying
   sentiment of those tweets in real-time"
   - Website URL (for attribution purposes only - if you do not have a
   personal website, then use the URL to your Twitter page, such as
   https://twitter.com/PacktPub)
   - Tell us how this app will be used (min 100 characters) e.g.
   "Internal training and development purposes only, including the
   deployment of machine learning models in real-time. It will not be
   visible to customers or 3rd parties."
   ```

4. Click the **Create** button to create your Twitter app.
5. Once your Twitter app has been created, navigate to the **Keys and Tokens** tab.
6. Make a note of your **Consumer API Key** and **Consumer API Secret Key** strings respectively.
7. Then click the **Create** button under **Access Token & Access Token Secret** to generate access tokens for your Twitter app. Set the access level to **Read-only** as this Twitter app will only read tweets, and will not generate any of its own.
8. Make a note of the resulting **Access Token** and **Access Token Secret** strings respectively.

The consumer API keys and access tokens will be used to provision our Python-based Kafka producer application read-only access to the stream of real-time tweets via the Twitter API, so it is important that you make a note of them.

Application configuration

We are now ready to start developing our end-to-end stream processing pipeline! First, let's create a configuration file in Python that will store all environmental and application-level options pertinent to our pipeline and local development node, as follows:

> The following Python configuration file, called `config.py`, can be found in the GitHub repository accompanying this book.

```python
#!/usr/bin/python

""" config.py: Environmental and Application Settings """

""" ENVIRONMENT SETTINGS """

# Apache Kafka
bootstrap_servers = '192.168.56.10:9092'
data_encoding = 'utf-8'

""" TWITTER APP SETTINGS """

consumer_api_key = 'Enter your Twitter App Consumer API Key here'
consumer_api_secret = 'Enter your Twitter App Consumer API Secret Key here'
access_token = 'Enter your Twitter App Access Token here'
access_token_secret = 'Enter your Twitter App Access Token Secret here'

""" SENTIMENT ANALYSIS MODEL SETTINGS """

# Name of an existing Kafka Topic to publish tweets to
twitter_kafka_topic_name = 'twitter'

# Keywords, Twitter Handle or Hashtag used to filter the Twitter Stream
twitter_stream_filter = '@British_Airways'

# Filesystem Path to the Trained Decision Tree Classifier
trained_classification_model_path = '..chapter06/models/airline-sentiment-
analysis-decision-tree-classifier'
```

This Python configuration file defines the following pertinent options:

- `bootstrap_servers`: A comma-delimited list of the hostname/IP address and port number pairings for the Kafka brokers. In our case, this is just the hostname/IP address of our single-node development environment at port `9092` by default.
- `consumer_api_key`: Enter the consumer API key associated with your Twitter app here.
- `consumer_api_secret`: Enter the consumer API secret key associated with your Twitter app here.
- `access_token`: Enter the access token associated with your Twitter app here.
- `access_token_secret`: Enter the access token secret associated with your Twitter app here.
- `twitter_kafka_topic_name`: The name of the Kafka topic to which our Kafka producer will publish tweets and from which our Structured Streaming Spark application will consume tweets.
- `twitter_stream_filter`: A keyword, Twitter handle, or hashtag to use in order to filter the stream of real-time tweets being captured from the Twitter API. In our case, we are filtering for real-time tweets directed at `@British_Airways`.
- `trained_classification_model_path`: The absolute path where we saved our trained decision tree classifier in `Chapter 6`, *Natural Language Processing Using Apache Spark*.

Kafka Twitter producer application

We are now ready to develop our Python-based Kafka producer application that will capture tweets about airlines that are being tweeted in real-time and then publish those tweets to the Apache Kafka `twitter` topic that we created previously. We will be using the following two Python libraries in order to develop our Kafka producer:

- `tweepy`: This library allows us to access the Twitter API programmatically using Python and the consumer API keys and access tokens that we generated earlier
- `pykafka`: This library allow us to instantiate a Python-based Apache Kafka client through which we can communicate and transact with our single-node Kafka cluster.

The following Python code file, called `kafka_twitter_producer.py`, can be found in the GitHub repository accompanying this book.

In regards to our Python-based Kafka producer application, we perform the following steps (numbered to correspond to the numbered comments in our Python code file):

1. First, we import the required modules from the `tweepy` and `pykafka` libraries respectively, as shown in the following code. We also import the configuration from our `config.py` file, which we created earlier:

```
import config
import tweepy
from tweepy import OAuthHandler
from tweepy import Stream
from tweepy.streaming import StreamListener
import pykafka
```

2. Next, we instantiate a `tweepy` wrapper for the Twitter API using the consumer API keys and access tokens defined in `config.py` to provide us authenticated and authorized programmatic access to the Twitter API, as follows:

```
auth = OAuthHandler(config.consumer_api_key,
    config.consumer_api_secret)
auth.set_access_token(config.access_token,
    config.access_token_secret)
api = tweepy.API(auth)
```

3. We then define a class in Python called `KafkaTwitterProducer`, which once instantiated, provides us with a `pykafka` client to our single-node Apache Kafka cluster, as shown in the following code. When this class is instantiated, it initially executes the code defined in the __init__ function, which creates a `pykafka` client using the bootstrap servers, the locations of which may be found in `config.py`. It then creates a Kafka producer that associates the producer to the `twitter_kafka_topic_name` Kafka topic also defined in `config.py`. When data is captured by our `pykafka` producer, the `on_data` function is invoked, which physically publishes the data to the Kafka topic.

If our `pykafka` producer encounters an error, then the `on_error` function is invoked, which, in our case, simply prints the error to the console and goes on to process the next message:

```
class KafkaTwitterProducer(StreamListener):

    def __init__(self):
        self.client = pykafka.KafkaClient(config.bootstrap_servers)
        self.producer = self.client.topics[bytes(
            config.twitter_kafka_topic_name,
            config.data_encoding)].get_producer()

    def on_data(self, data):
        self.producer.produce(bytes(data, config.data_encoding))
        return True

    def on_error(self, status):
        print(status)
        return True
```

4. Next, we instantiate a Twitter stream using the `Stream` module of the `tweepy` library. To achieve this, we simply pass our Twitter app authentication details and an instance of our `KafkaTwitterProducer` class to the Stream module:

```
print("Instantiating a Twitter Stream and publishing to the '%s'
    Kafka Topic..." % config.twitter_kafka_topic_name)
twitter_stream = Stream(auth, KafkaTwitterProducer())
```

5. Now that we have instantiated a Twitter stream, the final step is to filter the stream to deliver tweets of interest, based on the `twitter_stream_filter` option found in `config.py`, as shown in the following code:

```
print("Filtering the Twitter Stream based on the query '%s'..." %
    config.twitter_stream_filter)
twitter_stream.filter(track=[config.twitter_stream_filter])
```

We are now ready to run our Kafka producer application! Since it is a Python application, the easiest way to run it is simply to use the Linux command line, navigate to the directory containing `kafka_twitter_producer.py`, and execute it as follows:

```
> python kafka_twitter_producer.py
    $ Instantiating a Twitter Stream and publishing to the 'twitter'
    Kafka Topic...
    $ Filtering the Twitter Stream based on the query
    '@British_Airways'...
```

To check that it is actually capturing and publishing real-time tweets to Kafka, as described in Chapter 2, *Setting Up a Local Development Environment*, you can start a command-line consumer application to consume messages from the Twitter topic and print them to the console, as follows:

```
> cd {KAFKA_HOME}
> bin/kafka-console-consumer.sh --bootstrap-server 192.168.56.10:9092 --
topic twitter
```

Hopefully, you will see tweets printed to the console in real time. In our case, these tweets are all directed to "@British_Airways".

 The tweets themselves are captured via the Twitter API in JSON format, and contain not only the raw textual content of the tweet, but also associated metadata, such as the tweet ID, the username of the tweeter, the timestamp, and so on. For a full description of the JSON schema, please visit https://developer.twitter.com/en/docs/tweets/data-dictionary/overview/tweet-object.html.

Preprocessing and feature vectorization pipelines

As described earlier, in order to be able to apply our trained decision tree classifier to these real-time tweets, we first need to preprocess and vectorize them exactly as we did with our training and test datasets in Chapter 6, *Natural Language Processing Using Apache Spark*. However, rather than duplicating the preprocessing and vectorization pipeline logic within our Kafka consumer application itself, we will define our pipeline logic in a separate Python module and within Python *functions*. This way, any time we need to preprocess text as we did in Chapter 6, *Natural Language Processing Using Apache Spark*, we simply call the relevant Python function, thereby avoiding the need to duplicate the same code across different Python code files.

 The following Python code file, called model_pipelines.py, can be found in the GitHub repository accompanying this book.

In the following Python module, we define two functions. The first function applies the exact same pipeline of `MLlib` and `spark-nlp` feature transformers that we studied in Chapter 6, *Natural Language Processing Using Apache Spark,* in order to preprocess the raw textual content of the tweets. The second function then takes a preprocessed Spark dataframe and applies the HashingTF transformer to it in order to generate feature vectors based on term frequencies, exactly as we studied in Chapter 6, *Natural Language Processing Using Apache Spark.* The result is a Spark dataframe containing the original raw text of the tweet in a column called `text` and term frequency feature vectors in a column called `features`:

```python
#!/usr/bin/python

""" model_pipelines.py: Pre-Processing and Feature Vectorization Spark
Pipeline function definitions """

from pyspark.sql.functions import *
from pyspark.ml.feature import Tokenizer
from pyspark.ml.feature import StopWordsRemover
from pyspark.ml.feature import HashingTF
from pyspark.ml import Pipeline, PipelineModel

from sparknlp.base import *
from sparknlp.annotator import Tokenizer as NLPTokenizer
from sparknlp.annotator import Stemmer, Normalizer

def preprocessing_pipeline(raw_corpus_df):

    # Native MLlib Feature Transformers
    filtered_df = raw_corpus_df.filter("text is not null")
    tokenizer = Tokenizer(inputCol = "text", outputCol = "tokens_1")
    tokenized_df = tokenizer.transform(filtered_df)
    remover = StopWordsRemover(inputCol = "tokens_1",
       outputCol = "filtered_tokens")

    preprocessed_part_1_df = remover.transform(tokenized_df)
    preprocessed_part_1_df = preprocessed_part_1_df
       .withColumn("concatenated_filtered_tokens", concat_ws(" ",
          col("filtered_tokens")))

    # spark-nlp Feature Transformers
    document_assembler = DocumentAssembler()
       .setInputCol("concatenated_filtered_tokens")
    tokenizer = NLPTokenizer()
       .setInputCols(["document"]).setOutputCol("tokens_2")
    stemmer =
    Stemmer().setInputCols(["tokens_2"]).setOutputCol("stems")
```

```
    normalizer = Normalizer().setInputCols(["stems"])
        .setOutputCol("normalised_stems")

    preprocessing_pipeline = Pipeline(stages = [document_assembler,
        tokenizer, stemmer, normalizer])
    preprocessing_pipeline_model = preprocessing_pipeline
        .fit(preprocessed_part_1_df)
    preprocessed_df = preprocessing_pipeline_model
        .transform(preprocessed_part_1_df)
    preprocessed_df.select("id", "text", "normalised_stems")

    # Explode and Aggregate
    exploded_df = preprocessed_df
        .withColumn("stems", explode("normalised_stems"))
        .withColumn("stems", col("stems").getItem("result"))
        .select("id", "text", "stems")

    aggregated_df = exploded_df.groupBy("id")
        .agg(concat_ws(" ", collect_list(col("stems"))), first("text"))
        .toDF("id", "tokens", "text")
        .withColumn("tokens", split(col("tokens"), " ")
        .cast("array<string>"))

    # Return the final processed DataFrame
    return aggregated_df

def vectorizer_pipeline(preprocessed_df):

    hashingTF = HashingTF(inputCol = "tokens", outputCol = "features",
        numFeatures = 280)
    features_df = hashingTF.transform(preprocessed_df)

    # Return the final vectorized DataFrame
    return features_df
```

Kafka Twitter consumer application

We are finally ready to develop our Kafka consumer application using the Spark Structured Streaming engine in order to apply our trained decision tree classifier to the stream of real-time tweets in order to deliver real-time sentiment analysis!

 The following Python code file, called `kafka_twitter_consumer.py`, can be found in the GitHub repository accompanying this book.

In regards to our Spark Structured-Streaming-based Kafka consumer application, we perform the following steps (numbered to correspond to the numbered comments in our Python code file):

1. First, we import the configuration from our `config.py` file. We also import the Python functions containing the logic for our preprocessing and vectorization pipelines that we created earlier, as follows:

   ```
   import config
   import model_pipelines
   ```

2. Unlike our Jupyter notebook case studies, there is no need explicitly to instantiate a `SparkContext` as this will be done for us when we execute our Kafka consumer application via `spark-submit` in the command line. In this case study, we create a `SparkSession`, as shown in the following code that acts as an entry point into the Spark execution environment—even if it is already running—and which subsumes `SQLContext`. We can therefore use `SparkSession` to undertake the same SQL-like operations over data that we have seen previously, while still using the Spark Dataset/DataFrame API:

   ```
   spark = SparkSession.builder.appName("Stream Processing - Real-Time
   Sentiment Analysis").getOrCreate()
   ```

3. In this step, we load the decision tree classifier that we trained in Chapter 6, *Natural Language Processing Using Apache Spark*, (which used the *HashingTF* feature extractor) from the local filesystem into a `DecisionTreeClassificationModel` object so that we can apply it later on, as shown in the following code. Note that the absolute path to the trained decision tree classifier has been defined in `config.py`:

   ```
   decision_tree_model = DecisionTreeClassificationModel.load(
       config.trained_classification_model_path)
   ```

4. We are almost ready to start consuming messages from our single-node Kafka cluster. However, before doing so, we must note that Spark does not yet support the automatic inference and parsing of JSON key values into Spark dataframe columns. We must therefore explicitly define the JSON schema, or the subset of the JSON schema that we wish to retain, as follows:

```
schema = StructType([
    StructField("created_at", StringType()),
    StructField("id", StringType()),
    StructField("id_str", StringType()),
    StructField("text", StringType()),
    StructField("retweet_count", StringType()),
    StructField("favorite_count", StringType()),
    StructField("favorited", StringType()),
    StructField("retweeted", StringType()),
    StructField("lang", StringType()),
    StructField("location", StringType())
])
```

5. Now that we have defined our JSON schema, we are ready to start consuming messages. To do this, we invoke the `readStream` method on our `SparkSession` instance to consume streaming data. We specify that the source of our stream will be a Kafka cluster using the `format` method, after which we define the Kafka bootstrap servers and the name of the Kafka topic to which we want to subscribe, both of which have been defined in `config.py`. Finally, we invoke the `load` method to stream the latest messages consumed from the `twitter` topic to an unbounded Spark dataframe called `tweets_df`, as shown in the following code:

```
tweets_df = spark.readStream.format("kafka")
    .option("kafka.bootstrap.servers", config.bootstrap_servers)
    .option("subscribe", config.twitter_kafka_topic_name).load()
```

6. Records stored in a Kafka topic are persisted in binary format. In order to process the JSON representing our tweets, which are stored in a Kafka record under a field called `value`, we must first `CAST` the contents of `value` as a string. We then apply our defined schema to this JSON string and extract the fields of interest, as shown in the following code. In our case, we are only interested in the tweet ID, stored in the JSON key called `id`, and its raw textual content, stored in the JSON key called `text`. The resulting Spark dataframe will therefore have two string columns, `id` and `text`, containing these respective fields of interest:

```
tweets_df = tweets_df.selectExpr(
    "CAST(key AS STRING)", "CAST(value AS STRING) as json")
```

```
.withColumn("tweet", from_json(col("json"), schema=schema))
.selectExpr("tweet.id_str as id", "tweet.text as text")
```

7. Now that we have consumed raw tweets from our Kafka topic and parsed them into a Spark dataframe, we can apply our preprocessing pipeline as we did in Chapter 6, *Natural Language Processing Using Apache Spark*. However, rather than duplicating the same code from Chapter 6, *Natural Language Processing Using Apache Spark*, into our Kafka consumer application, we simply call the relevant function that we defined in `model_pipelines.py`, namely `preprocessing_pipeline()`, as shown in the following code. This preprocessing pipeline tokenizes the raw text, removes stop words, applies a stemming algorithm, and normalizes the resulting tokens:

```
preprocessed_df = model_pipelines.preprocessing_pipeline(tweets_df)
```

8. Next, we generate feature vectors from these tokens, as we did in Chapter 6, *Natural Language Processing Using Apache Spark*. We call the `vectorizer_pipeline()` function from `model_pipelines.py` to generate feature vectors based on term frequencies, as shown in the following code. The resulting Spark dataframe, called `features_df`, contains three pertinent columns, namely `id` (raw tweet ID), `text` (raw tweet text), and `features` (term-frequency feature vectors):

```
features_df = model_pipelines.vectorizer_pipeline(preprocessed_df)
```

9. Now that we have generated feature vectors from our stream of tweets, we can apply our trained decision tree classifier to this stream in order to predict and classify their underlying sentiment. We do this as normal, by invoking the `transform` method on the `features_df` dataframe, resulting in a new Spark dataframe called `predictions_df`, containing the columns `id` and `text` as before, and a new column called `prediction` that contains our predicted classification, as shown in the following code. As described in Chapter 6, *Natural Language Processing Using Apache Spark*, a prediction of 1 implies non-negative sentiment, and a prediction of 0 implies negative sentiment:

```
predictions_df = decision_tree_model.transform(features_df)
    .select("id", "text", "prediction")
```

10. Finally, we write our predicted results dataframe to an output sink. In our case, we define the output sink as simply the console that is used to execute the Kafka consumer PySpark application—that is, the console from which we execute `spark-submit`. We achieve this by invoking the `writeStream` method on the relevant Spark dataframe and stating `console` as the `format` of choice. We start our output stream by invoking the `start` method, and invoke the `awaitTermination` method, which tells Spark to continue processing our streaming pipeline indefinitely until it is explicitly interrupted and stopped, as follows:

```
query = predictions_df.writeStream
    .outputMode("complete")
    .format("console")
    .option("truncate", "false")
    .start()
query.awaitTermination()
```

Note that the `outputMode` method defines what gets written to the output sink, and can take one of the following options:

- `complete`: The entire (updated) results table is written to the output sink
- `append`: Only the new rows appended to the results table since the last trigger is written to the output sink
- `update`: Only the rows that were updated in the results table since the last trigger is written to the output sink

We are now ready to run our Kafka consumer application! Since it is a Spark application, we can execute it via *spark-submit* on the Linux command line. To do this, navigate to the directory where we installed Apache Spark (see Chapter 2, *Setting Up a Local Development Environment*). Thereafter we can execute the `spark-submit` program by passing to it the following command-line arguments:

- `--master`: The Spark master URL.
- `--packages`: The third-party libraries and dependencies required for the given Spark application to work. In our case, our Kafka consumer application is dependent on the availability of two third-party libraries, namely `spark-sql-kafka` (Spark Kafka integration) and `spark-nlp` (NLP algorithms, as studied in Chapter 6, *Natural Language Processing Using Apache Spark*).

- `--py-files`: Since our Kafka consumer is a PySpark application, we can use this argument to pass a comma-delimited list of filesystem paths to any Python code files that our application is dependent on. In our case, our Kafka consumer application is dependent on `config.py` and `model_pipelines.py` respectively.
- The final argument is the path to the Python code file containing our Spark Structured Streaming driver program, in our case, `kafka_twitter_consumer.py`

The final commands to execute therefore look as follows:

```
> cd {SPARK_HOME}
> bin/spark-submit --master spark://192.168.56.10:7077 --packages
org.apache.spark:spark-sql-kafka-0-10_2.11:2.3.2,JohnSnowLabs:spark-
nlp:1.7.0 --py-files chapter08/config.py,chapter08/model_pipelines.py
chapter08/kafka_twitter_consumer.py
```

Assuming that the Python-based Kafka producer application is running as well, the results table should periodically be written to the console and contain the real-time prediction and classification of the underlying sentiment behind the stream of airline tweets being consumed by the Twitter API from across the world and written by real Twitter users! A selection of real-world classified tweets that was processed when filtering using "`@British_Airways`" is shown in the following table:

Tweet Raw Contents	Predicted Sentiment
@British_Airways @HeathrowAirport I mean I'm used to cold up in Shetland but this is a whole different kind of cold!!	Non-negative
@British_Airways have just used the app to check-in for our flight bari to lgw but the app shows no hold luggage	Negative
She looks more Beautiful at Night	A380 takeoff London Heathrow @HeathrowAviYT @HeathrowAirport @British_Airways	Non-negative
The @British_Airways #B747 landing into @HeathrowAirport	Non-negative
@British_Airways trying to check in online for my flight tomorrow and receiving a 'sorry we are unable to offer you online check-in for this flight' message. Any idea why??	Negative

Summary

In this chapter, we developed Apache Kafka producer and consumer applications and utilized Spark's Structured Streaming engine to process streaming data consumed from a Kafka topic. In our real-world case study, we designed, developed, and deployed an end-to-end stream processing pipeline that was capable of consuming real tweets being authored across the world and then classified their underlying sentiment using machine learning, all of which was done in real time.

In this book, we went on both a theoretical and a hands-on journey through some of the most important and exciting technologies and frameworks that underpin the data-intelligence-driven revolution being seen across industry today. We started out by describing a new breed of distributed and scalable technologies that allow us to store, process, and analyze huge volumes of structured, semi-structured, and unstructured data. Using these technologies as a base, we established the context for artificial intelligence and how it relates to machine learning and deep learning. We then went on to explore some of the key concepts in, and applications of, machine learning, including supervised learning, unsupervised learning, natural language processing, and deep learning. We illustrated these key concepts through a wide variety of relevant and exciting use cases that were implemented using our big data processing engine of choice—Apache Spark. Finally, because timely decisions are critical to many businesses and organizations in the modern world, we extended our deployment of machine learning models beyond batch processing to real-time streaming applications!

Other Books You May Enjoy

If you enjoyed this book, you may be interested in these other books by Packt:

Apache Spark Deep Learning Cookbook
Ahmed Sherif

ISBN: 9781788474221

- Set up a fully functional Spark environment
- Understand practical machine learning and deep learning concepts
- Apply built-in machine learning libraries within Spark
- Explore libraries that are compatible with TensorFlow and Keras
- Explore NLP models such as word2vec and TF-IDF on Spark
- Organize dataframes for deep learning evaluation
- Apply testing and training modeling to ensure accuracy
- Access readily available code that may be reusable

Apache Spark 2.x Machine Learning Cookbook
Siamak Amirghodsi

ISBN: 9781783551606

- Get to know how Scala and Spark go hand-in-hand for developers when developing ML systems with Spark
- Build a recommendation engine that scales with Spark
- Find out how to build unsupervised clustering systems to classify data in Spark
- Build machine learning systems with the Decision Tree and Ensemble models in Spark
- Deal with the curse of high-dimensionality in big data using Spark
- Implement Text analytics for Search Engines in Spark
- Streaming Machine Learning System implementation using Spark

Leave a review - let other readers know what you think

Please share your thoughts on this book with others by leaving a review on the site that you bought it from. If you purchased the book from Amazon, please leave us an honest review on this book's Amazon page. This is vital so that other potential readers can see and use your unbiased opinion to make purchasing decisions, we can understand what our customers think about our products, and our authors can see your feedback on the title that they have worked with Packt to create. It will only take a few minutes of your time, but is valuable to other potential customers, our authors, and Packt. Thank you!

Index

results 189
spark-submit program 188
ImageNet
  reference 184
Inception-v3
  reference 184
integrated development environments (IDE) 55
inverse document frequency (IDF) 157

J

Java Development Kit (JDK) 51
Java Virtual Machines (JVM) 51
JavaScript Object Notation (JSON) format 21
Jupyter Notebook
  about 56
  reference 57
  starting 56
  troubleshooting 57

K

k-means clustering
  about 121, 125
  brain tumors, detecting 125
  case study, brain tumor detection 125
  image segmentation 127
  images, converting into numerical feature vectors
    126
  in Apache Spark 128, 131, 134
  k-means cost function 127
knowledge discovery 71
KSQL
  reference 196

L

lemmatisation 84
linear regression
  about 89
  case study, bike sharing demand prediction 90
  multivariate linear regression 99
  univariate linear regression 91
logistic regression
  about 103
  case study, breast cancer prediction 108, 110,
    112
  confusion matrix 105

receiver operator characteristic curve 106
  threshold value 104
loss function 80, 169

M

machine learning
  about 68
  pipelines, in Apache Spark 85, 87
  reinforced learning 72
  supervised learning 69, 70
  unsupervised learning 71
magnetic resonance imaging (MR) 125
Manhattan distance 122
matrix multiplication 180
maximum coordinate distance 122
micro-batch processing 36
MLlib
  reference 40
MongoDB
  reference 18
mono-layer or single-layer ANNs 80
multi-layer ANNs 80
multilayer perceptron (MLP)
  about 164
  hidden layers 165, 168
  in Apache Spark 173, 175
  input layer 165
  multilayer perceptron classifier (MLPC) 165
  output layer 168, 169
multivariate linear regression
  about 99
  correlation 100
  in Apache Spark 100, 102

N

natural language processing (NLP) 72, 83
node 79
normalization
  reference 125
NoSQL databases
  about 19
  CAP theorem 25, 27
  columnar databases 21
  document databases 21
  graph databases 23

key-value databases 23

O

OCR
about 170
classification, output layer 173
input data 170
patterns, detecting in hidden layer 172
training architecture 171
online transaction processing (OLTP) 21
Open Images v4 dataset 191
overfitting 100

P

padding 180
Pay-As-You-Go (PAYG) 40
pooling algorithms
max pooling 182
preprocessing pipeline
about 146
lemmatization techniques 147
normalization techniques 148
stemming technique 147
stop words techniques 147
tokenization technique 147
principal component analysis (PCA)
about 134
case study, movie recommendation system 135
covariance matrix 137
eigenvalues 141
eigenvectors 138, 141
identity matrix 138
in Apache Spark 141, 143
principal components 136
property graph 24

R

random forests
about 117
K-Fold cross validation 117, 119
real-time sentiment analysis
about 200
application configuration 203
feature vectorization pipelines 207
Kafka 201

Kafka Servers 201
Kafka Twitter consumer application 210, 214
Kafka Twitter producer application 204, 207
preprocessing 207
Twitter API 202
Twitter apps 202
Twitter developer account 202
Zookeeper, starting 201
receiver operator characteristic (ROC)
about 106
area 107
Red Hat Enterprise Linux (RHEL) 50
reference logical architecture
about 42
data insights 45
data intelligence layer 45
data processing layer 44
data sources layer 43
Governance and Security 46
Hardware and Software 47
Management, Administration, and Orchestration 46
Network and Access Middleware 46
persistent data storage layer 43
reporting layer 45
serving data storage layer 44
unified access layer 45
regression algorithms
examples 70
reinforced learning
about 72
reference 72
relational database management systems (RDBMSes) 8
resilient distributed datasets (RDDs)
about 32
actions 32
transformations 32
root mean square error (RMSE) 93

S

sentiment analysis
about 150
NLP pipeline 151
NLP, in Apache Spark 152, 154, 157, 160, 161

sharding 8
sigmoid activation function 167
single-layer perceptron (SLP) 164
single-node cluster
  technologies 49
spark-tree-plotting
  reference 116
sparkdl
  reference 184
stages, for real-time sentiment analysis
  Kafka consumer 200
  Kafka producer 200
  output sink 201
  Stream processor and MLlib 200
  trained decision tree classifier 200
standard output (stdout) 201
stemming 84
stream processing 36
stream processing APIs
  Spark Streaming (DStreams) 197
  Spark Streaming (DStreams), reference 197
  Structured Streaming 197
  Structured Streaming, reference 197
Structured Query Language (SQL) 10
Sum of Squared Errors (SSE) 93
supervised learning 69

T

TensorFlow
  reference 40, 184
terabytes (TB) 15
term frequency (TF) 157
term frequency–inverse document
  frequency(TF–IDF) 149, 150
The Cancer Imaging Archive (TCIA)
  reference 128
tokenization 84

transfer learning process 187
transformers 85
true positive rate (TPR) 106, 110
Twitter developer account
  reference 202

U

unit 79
univariate linear regression
  about 91, 92
  in Apache Spark 94, 95, 98
  R-squared 93
  residuals 93
  root mean square error (RMSE) 93
University of California's (UCI) machine
  reference 90
unsupervised learning 71
use cases, NLP
  machine translation and transcription 84
  Named entity recognition (NER) 83
  question answering 84
  relationship extraction 84
  searching 84
  sentiment analysis 84
User Interface (UI) 61
user-defined functions (UDFs)
  NLP, in Apache Spark 152

V

variance 137
vertical scaling 8
virtualization software
  Oracle VirtualBox 50
  VMWare Workstation Player 50
Visual Basic for Applications (VBA) 10
Visual Studio Code (VS Code)
  reference 56

Lightning Source UK Ltd.
Milton Keynes UK
UKHW032009301218
334744UK00004B/124/P